PRAISE FOR LIFEBLOOD

"An honest and transparent look at a biblical truth that needs to be heard in our day."

—Joel Arndt
Senior Pastor, Community Alliance Church, Detroit Lakes, MN

"John is a seasoned writer who passes along a great deal of wisdom in understandable ways through his work in *Lifeblood*. He gives honest, relatable perspectives about what it means for us to fully devote our lives to Christ—and why that devotion requires decisions every day to fully commit to Him. This book is especially for people who find themselves in a spiritual rut and in need of help to get back on track."

—Matthew Branaugh
Editor, *Christianity Today*

"Since I first encountered it, I've enjoyed John Brandon's writing. So I'm naturally excited about this new project—and all the more so that John is exploring one of the most important topics imaginable. His full-orbed, Christ-filled vision for the Christian life is compelling, and his writing is energetic."

—Aaron Cline Hanbury
Editorial Director, *Relevant* magazine

"Read John Brandon's *Lifeblood* at your own risk! If you dare to read it, you'll be challenged to open the throttle wide for Jesus. A refreshing and challenging read in a day when so many are choosing the path of least resistance!"

—David Johnson
Senior Pastor, River of Life Church, Elk River, MN

"John Brandon is among Inc.com's standout columnists. His pieces are consistently well-written, popular with our audience, and a good read. He's very knowledgeable and resourceful. On a personal level, John is a pleasure to work with and a favorite among our writers. I love working with him!"

—Laura Lorber

Executive Editor, *Inc.* magazine

"John Brandon has written an inspiring and practical book about what it means to be truly connected with God, leading you through what it means to be consumed by Christ to the point where it is in your lifeblood."

—Jeremy Moulton

Marketing Director, Camp Shamineau, Motley, MN

LIFEBLOOD

LIFEBLOOD

TAPPING INTO JESUS AS THE
TRUE SOURCE OF RENEWAL

JOHN BRANDON

CLC PUBLICATIONS
Fort Washington, PA 19034

Lifeblood
Published by CLC Publications

U.S.A.
P.O. Box 1449, Fort Washington, PA 19034

UNITED KINGDOM
CLC International (UK)
Unit 5, Glendale Avenue, Sandycroft, Flintshire, CH5 2QP

Printed in the United States of America

ISBN (paperback): 978-1-61958-276-7
ISBN (e-book): 978-1-61958-277-4

Italics in Scripture quotations are the emphasis of the author.

Cover design by Mitch Bolton.

DEDICATION

For Rebecca

ACKNOWLEDGMENTS

The cabin smelled like the windows had not been opened in three months. My family had relocated to this pristine location in Minnesota, a temporary residence after we sold our house in a town nearby. I held my nose when I walked inside the first time, even though I was grateful for the shelter. Then my wife came up with the brilliant idea of writing out in the garage. For an entire month, I sat in a chair with a desk and a laptop, looking out over a few pine trees—surrounded by lawn mowers, Weedwackers, and moving boxes.

My "day job" is writing a column for *Inc.* magazine, but one day I hit the wall—hard. I couldn't think of anything to say. I kept going back to the cabin for coffee, then trudging over to my makeshift office—singing praises to God that I didn't have to deal with the cabin smell but curious about my sudden writer's block. I decided to try something completely different.

It turns out, you're holding it in your hands right now. That "something different" was a chapter of a book, which became an entire book. I realized that morning in the garage that I was trying to do things under my own power. But God-sized pursuits require God-sized power. Our efforts must be a result of the changes and molding that occur inside our hearts. I knew that.

I also knew I needed help from family and friends. My wife, Rebecca, was the main motivator, the champion who kept telling me to write, write, write. My Uncle Richard Burt helped me with editing from an early stage. My friend Tim, who met me for breakfast at a small town diner for over five years, was a sounding board for me every week. Some of the ideas you'll find in this book were sharpened over eggs and bacon, dark roast coffee, and dad jokes.

During the fall of 2016, while writing the original manuscript, I found my true calling. I started mentoring college students around December of that year and set aside all aspirations for achieving acclaim as a writer. (I also set aside a higher paycheck.) My goals and motivations changed. *Lifeblood* is really a gift to the students who helped me find that calling—to Josie and Seth and Michaela and Josiah, to Kaylyn and Robin, and many others. Crown College has helped me practice what it means to nurture others. Thank you.

My kids also played a huge role. They let me be their dad. Rachel, Hannah, Joshua, and Katie all put up with my bad moods and cranky comments. My two sons-in-law, Jonas and Eddie, are also closely aligned in spirit, wonderful blessings both. My family is a testing ground for many of the ideas in *Lifeblood*, as untested and raw as they were. The spiritual changes inside of me became actions in front of my kids, for better or worse. In the end, it was seeing their reactions that helped me identify where God needs to keep molding me into His image.

During the editing and revision process, I relocated for a week at a time to write and ponder deep spiritual thoughts on an island located near Motley, Minnesota. It's owned by Camp Shamineau, where my kids all worked as counselors, and I write about the camp director in this book. My friend Jeremy Moulton let me use the cabin. I found a way to keep warm on my own.

Even the folks who owned that smelly cabin (since restored) found the time to read this book and helped with editing. In the end, it wasn't me at all. *Lifeblood* is one of those books that works much better as an outpouring of mind and soul, a living and breathing example of how an inner life focused on serving a Savior can produce an outward abundance. When that happens, it's hard to give credit to anyone other than my Lord—working in my own life, molding me to become a better servant and to find His purpose. To God be the glory!

CONTENTS

1

THE LIFEBLOOD IN OUR PERSONAL LIVES

I was swimming by myself in the Boundary Waters Canoe Area in northern Minnesota. My college roommate had suggested we take a camping trip together, but he liked to sleep in. I liked to do things impulsively.

Hypothermia is not fun. Ask anyone who has suffered from it and you will get an earful. When you have it, your arms feel like logs. Your legs go catatonic. That's what happened to me just ten feet from shore on a warm, sunny morning. I felt as though I was about to sink. I gasped for air. I questioned my decision-making ability.

I had a few interesting (and what seemed like final) thoughts:

How did this happen?

Why didn't I bring a rope?

Look at those clouds!

I wondered if my last thoughts on this blue spinning orb would be so surreal and random that I'd be thinking about how the clouds looked like bunny ears. I wondered if my roommate was still asleep. And I started to really hate the Boundary Waters.

Hypothermia is a fairly common problem in the great northern area of Minnesota, just below Canada. The lakes in this area are particularly chilly, even in the middle of summer.

Here are a few scientific facts about hypothermia. First, when you have it, your body starts to lose heat faster than you can produce it. Doesn't sound good, does it? Also, your blood starts to congeal, and you can't think clearly. In fact, when you have hypothermia, you don't even realize you have it. That's the most dangerous part because it feels as if you're just fine.

After a few seconds of experiencing the abovementioned symptoms, I yelled. Then I yelled again. I edged closer to shore. My body felt heavy. Things didn't look good.

I floated for a while, and then looked up. My friend was peering down at me with a quizzical expression. He had appeared out of nowhere and he reached out to help. I somehow managed to lunge forward and grab his hand. He pulled me up to a rock outcropping and made a joke about picking the wrong time to go swimming. I couldn't talk. I just sat down and felt numb.

"You okay there, John?" he asked laughingly in his thick Kentucky accent.

Not really. I had never experienced anything like that. It took me a few hours to recover, although I wonder now if I was as close to death as I'd felt at the time. All I knew was my body was not cooperating with my mind. I wasn't able to get my arms and legs to propel me toward the shore. I couldn't do what I wanted to do because I didn't have the ability or the strength. My thoughts were clouded. I knew the goal—to get to the shore, climb out of the water, eat breakfast—but I was sinking fast.

I wonder at times if the spiritual life is like that. I wonder if it is *exactly* like that. Our lives don't match up with our ambitions. We know what we want to do and we set goals, but our behavior does not always align with those goals. We aren't even aware that we're sinking when our commitment to Christ starts to falter. Is there anything we can do about that? There are a few pat answers, of course. We can read the Bible more. Pray. Find other like-minded Christians. Sadly, these simple answers to complex questions don't always work, do they? The Bible seems stale. Our prayer lives are routine. People in church act like jerks. Between periods of total isolation and loneliness, we get distracted by the allure of worldly things—and I'm talking about more than just the iPhone. We're sinking either because we're alone and we have no one to save us, or we don't quite realize that our blood is congealing. It's like we don't even know we have spiritual hypothermia, even though many of the signs are present. We try to do things in our own strength. We share our faith with others, but we're not even sure our own faith is strong.

I know all about this because I tend to have these struggles myself. Some days, I can't find Bible passages that make me go, "Wow," the way they did before. I pray with my wife, Rebecca, nearly every day, but some days I'm guilty of dropping the ball—I just skip our prayer time and go to work. Some Sundays I struggle to find deep relationships at church and deeper meaning in the message. This struggle has a generational name. A few years ago, the phrase "the done" came to describe people who were done with church but still called themselves Christians.

There are no easy answers to this problem. As with everything important in life, it is hard to deal with spiritual deadness and break out of spiritual patterns we've developed over decades.

Change takes effort. Yet we can find joy in our spiritual lives. We can find life again. The secret is in the blood.

I have a confession to make. I really hate flying. It's not that I have any fears about crashing into the side of a mountain and bursting into a ball of flames. I don't even mind the stress of flight delays or screaming babies. As hard as this is to admit, the reason air travel is so annoying to me is because I tend to be a controller. I hate waiting. But I don't have a choice. If my flight leaves at seven, it's not like I can walk up to the attendant and insist the pilot leave earlier so I can get to my destination faster.

I imagine such a conversation would go something like this:

ME: My laptop died and I'm a little bored. Can we leave an hour early?

ATTENDANT AT THE DESK: *Stares blankly into empty space.*

ME: No, really. Most of us are here already. Shouldn't we get a head start?

ATTENDANT: *Considers picking up the phone and calling security.*

ME: Okay, I'll just go find a smoothie instead.

On one business trip, I was particularly agitated as I sat on the plane waiting to take off for Boston. Maybe I was unhappy with the interior decor of the jet or the novel a preteen next to me was reading. Maybe I was just hungry. When the pilot announced a slight departure delay, I felt personally offended. Was the airline not aware that I was on board? Had they even checked the manifest? When our plane finally pulled back from the gate, I decided (uncharacteristically) to pay attention to the announcements. Maybe I thought they'd be soothing. A few of the instructions seemed a bit simplistic: *My seat can act as a flotation device? So can my sofa at home. We have to keep our seat belts fastened? Tell that to the executive next to me who thinks it's very optional.*

Then the attendant said something profound. She mentioned how, in the event of a water landing, we should always fit the oxygen mask over our own mouths before assisting anyone else. Søren Kierkegaard had nothing on this woman. She could have taught a class on advanced philosophy at any university on the planet.

Her comment got me thinking. How often do we try to live like that as Christians, as if we are not primarily responsible for our own spiritual condition? We tend to assume our growth is a result of external circumstances, even to the point that we criticize the worship time or the sermon in church when we feel a little cheated. How dare the pastor deliver a half-hearted message when that thirty-minute period is when I'm not checking Facebook and I'm open to what God has to say? Does anyone around here realize I had to get up earlier than usual this morning?

Yet Jesus gave us this simple command in Luke 10:27 for a reason: "'Love the Lord your God with all your heart and with all your soul and with all your strength and with all your mind'; and, 'Love your neighbor as yourself.'" Who knew, right? Our personal growth starts with loving God. That's a recipe for spiritual success.

It's backed up nicely by Hebrews 12:11–13.

> All discipline for the moment seems not to be joyful, but sorrowful; yet to those who have been trained by it, afterwards it yields the peaceful fruit of righteousness.
>
> Therefore, strengthen the hands that are weak and the knees that are feeble, and make straight paths for your feet, so that *the limb* which is lame may not be

> put out of joint, but rather be healed. (Heb. 12:11–13, NASB).

A close reading of this passage reveals that it's talking about our own spiritual condition. We have to get healthy first before we can help anyone else. (In case you're wondering, that's also the passage you can use to justify a spiritual retreat to Colorado with your wife and let your kids wonder why they're not invited.) It's okay for us to focus on ourselves. It's called finding strength so we can walk. It's called making our paths straight. We need to make the path straight for our feet. We need to fit the oxygen mask over our own mouths.

Has anyone ever questioned why you're taking an extended break? People seem to forget that even Jesus retreated to the woods to find solitude. (If they'd had Caribou Coffee back then, he would have ordered the coffee cake and the big mug—the one you can refill for free.)

Think about how the "oxygen mask on you first" principle works in marriage or friendship or raising kids. As Louie Giglio, pastor of Atlanta's Passion City Church, has explained in his messages, our primary concern when considering a future spouse is to prepare ourselves to be the person someone else wants to marry, not to think we are so amazing that we get our pick. Jesus said we are supposed to love God first. We're supposed to figure out how to become better conduits of His grace, first and foremost. The truth is, God cares about our spiritual growth; and the person we marry or a new friend should help us *grow* the most, not be the person who meets all our needs. For some reason, young adults don't always understand this. When they were younger, my kids (mostly my three girls, but also my son) used to talk about how they thought there was one special person out there for them. They perceived a spouse as someone God had specifically selected out of a billion available options. Instead, it's better to be that person. The greatest fulfillment I've found in marriage is in having my wife sit me down and tell me the truth about myself and set me straight, even though it isn't easy or fun. My best friends in life have been those who were not afraid to chew me out. In a church context, I've found the most connection with people who show love in ways that are not always perfectly smooth.

Here's a good example of how this works. My wife always knows when I'm cranky. Usually the solution is to give me food. That seems to work. When I work too hard and get distracted, she knows my body is experiencing a serious lack of protein. I must have a certain look that says "needs pizza" that she can spot from a mile away. Yet if I really want to be the husband she wants me to be, it might be a good idea for me to eat more regularly. I need to fit the oxygen mask over my own face before I try to help her.

You may question this logic. Having a "me first" mentality is selfish, right? Don't we grow more by serving others? Doesn't the Bible say in Matthew 10:39 that we have to lose our lives first? Isn't it all about sacrifice? It's easy to forget the last part of that verse: "Whoever finds their life will lose it, and whoever loses their life for my sake will find it." The secret is in finding our lives. That's the first step in learning to depend on lifeblood.

The idea of sacrificing our own physical needs may make sense at first, but we tend to shift that thinking too quickly and assume that the strong Christians are the ones who forgo their personal growth and get busy doing the Lord's work. They serve, but then they falter.

Giving up physical needs and then immediately trying to serve doesn't work. Our growth stalls because we forget that the basic building blocks of spiritual maturity happen in the quiet moments of our daily relationship with God. If we forget about Jesus, we forget the basic truth of Christianity: We are to love Him first with all of our hearts, souls, strength, and minds, and then we are to love others. It's in that order for a specific reason—to equip us properly.

The solution is to tap into the *lifeblood*, which *English Oxford Living Dictionaries* defines as "the indispensable factor or influence that gives something its strength and vitality." *Indispensable* sounds like a good name for a Chris Tomlin song (since he seems to love one-word song titles that describe God; seriously, look up his hits). It's the indwelling of the Spirit that provides the power we need for Christian living. That's where we'll truly find the strength we need.

As we will see over the course of this book, the lifeblood is critically important. That's why Paul said this in Colossians 1:29: "For this I toil, struggling with all his energy that he powerfully works within me" (ESV). Even Paul—who wrote much of the New Testament—was keenly aware that spiritual maturity was all about how much we allow the power of Christ to change us and then rely on that power to help us in ministry and life.

It's hard though, isn't it? The reason so many Christians struggle to grow in their faith, the reason they fight habitual sin, the reason they just attend church rather than connect with other believers on a deep emotional level is that they are faking their way through the Christian life. Our hearts change when we confess Christ, but they also change day by day when we seek Him consistently. And I don't mean morning devotions for only five minutes. The idea with lifeblood is that we swim out into the deep end of our faith because we are having personal communion with Christ, so we begin abiding with Him in the wellspring of our daily routines. It means our every word and action flows from this fellowship, not from our own effort. When we commit to this kind of communion, our actions reflect our reliance on God's power.

It's amazing how many Christians don't spend time with God. We get a little conceited, and we get bored reading the Bible each day. But when this happens, our view of the spiritual disciplines is rooted in false thinking. We think the disciplines themselves will help us grow; we don't realize that the disciplines must always have a root in a relationship with our Savior, which is the critical component of this communion. In fact, it's possible to read a seminal book like Richard Foster's *Celebration of Discipline*, nod in agreement, meet in a study group, announce you are a prayer warrior, and even attempt to follow the instructions about prayer and fasting (among other things), but make it all a rote or purely intellectual exercise. What's missing? Utter devotion to our Savior. Life-changing faith in Jesus.

That is what's so great about lifeblood thinking. It's not about a scheduled activity. It's not about a scripted prayer. It's not about a Sunday service ritual. It's 100 percent total abandonment to a deep and abiding relationship with Christ that always takes center stage. We can't wait to get up in the morning and meet with Jesus because we need the spiritual energy. We can't wait to go to church because we need a message of hope. We can't wait to go out on the mission field and share our faith because it was renewed that very morning. It's not about "let go and let God."

It's let God, then go.

The opposite of this thought process—doing everything in our own strength instead—is a little frightening and much too common. We connect with people at church because we're amazingly gifted socially, or we lead worship because we have a voice like an angel. We even read books (not this one though!) looking for conviction that will cause us to make changes and become a little more serious about serving, tithing more of our money, or loving others. These aren't bad things unless we focus only on the action. The phrase "there is power in the blood" means that the power comes from Christ's blood—*it* is our source of spiritual strength. Too often we focus on the action because that's what we can control. We see the immediate outcome.

I've lived that. I've picked up Christian books with the intention of being convicted enough to do something different in my life and somehow change my attitude about Christianity. It's an act of desperation, yet it's still an act—it's still something I'm trying to do instead of just seeking more communion with Christ. Yes, it's important to think about our motivations: Do we really want to learn more? Do we want to be convicted? Do we want to act differently? Do we want to think purer thoughts? Do we want to attain a new level of maturity? But all the things we try to do to grow in our faith pale in comparison to just finding a deeper bond with God. All the knowledge we can accumulate fails in comparison to developing an abiding love for our Savior. Then, when we tap in deeply, we are propelled by Him, not ourselves.

How does that work? In many ways, it starts with an intentional attitude. When we cross the threshold of our churches, we should go with the attitude that we have a deep desire to tap into the lifeblood. We are there to put on our own oxygen masks, then help everyone else with theirs after we have the power to actually impact them through Christ. We must see our personal lives, marriages, families, jobs, and churches as opportunities for us to both receive and show spiritual depth. It starts with us changing our perspectives about why we are even doing spiritual things in the first place, and is followed by actions that come from true devotion to God. That's the sign of a changed heart.

Many Christians don't like to talk about the blood of Jesus. It sounds weird. In fact, I know a few Christians who don't even like to talk about Communion. A few chalk it up as an ancient ritual or an old-world superstition, something that doesn't apply anymore. They say that it's better to see Communion as a thought. You should *remember* Christ's death and resurrection. They leave out the bread and the wine (aka the grape juice). Jesus didn't really intend for us to see any real meaning behind it, they say. We're not supposed to drink anything or eat anything. Communion is more of a concept than a practice. It's no longer relevant.

I understand why people get grossed out by the idea of the body and the blood. When we read the Communion passage in First Corinthians 11:23–26, it does seem a bit outdated, even strange.

> I received from the Lord what I also passed on to you: The Lord Jesus, on the night he was betrayed, took bread, and when he had given thanks, he broke it and said, "This is my body, which is for you; do this in remembrance of me." In the same way, after supper he took the cup, saying, "This cup is the new

> covenant in my blood; do this, whenever you drink it, in remembrance of me." For whenever you eat this bread and drink this cup, you proclaim the Lord's death. (1 Cor. 11:23–26)

Wait, really? Drink the blood? Eat the body? For this reason, early Christians were called cannibals. It's true that the blood of Jesus is found all over the New Testament as a reminder of His sacrifice for us on the cross. But there is a second meaning that's more than mere remembrance, more than something we look back on with a fond memory. The blood of Jesus is supposed to be life changing, and that life-changing communion is supposed to happen daily. It's not a ritual. It's a way to live our lives.

What if Jesus was serious in John 6:56 when He said we are to drink His blood? He wasn't *that* serious—we're not supposed to be vampires. The story behind consuming the blood of Christ has a deeper meaning. No, we don't take the blood as a way to earn salvation. Rather, we are supposed to live as though we are exchanging our blood for His. We're supposed to act out of a changed heart, not act without first seeking Him with our whole hearts. We're supposed to actually rely on the blood of Jesus. The act of remembering is profound. But it is even more profound when we remember *daily*, which is what some of us have lost in our Christian journeys.

A believer once told me he was surprised that people would reduce the Christian life to simple daily devotions and prayer. He insisted that true maturity is more about learning the advanced teachings of Scripture. What he seemed to forget is that this "simple" devotional and prayer life is where we develop maturity. We're meeting with the God of the universe over coffee.

That's more important than anything.

The whole passage from John 6:53–57 explains it all.

> Jesus said to them, "Very truly I tell you, unless you eat the flesh of the Son of Man and drink his blood, you have no life in you. Whoever eats my flesh and drinks my blood has eternal life, and I will raise them up at the last day. For my flesh is real food and my blood is real drink. Whoever eats my flesh and drinks my blood remains in me, and I in them. Just as the living Father sent me and I live because of the Father, so the one who feeds on me will live because of me."

Do you have this life in you? Do you have this lifeblood? That's what this book is about. The lifeblood is about more than just an act of remembering. It's about living as though we actually believe what we are trying to remember. Lifeblood living is also more than praying a prayer of salvation. It's praying daily to live as though we have Christ's blood flowing inside of us. The lifeblood is more than a song. It's something profound coursing through our veins in such a way that we can't help but be wholly devoted to the One who gave us this lifeblood in the first place.

In addition, lifeblood living is an exchange. We need a daily transfusion, not just on Sundays and not just when we happen to pull out a Bible and read a verse. We get caught in this trap of thinking about the blood only when we take Communion or when the pastor at church talks about Jesus dying on the cross for our sins.

That's dangerous because it's too easy for us to go back to old patterns—we battle temptation, we try to do good, and we crack open the Bible on occasion. We don't accept the possibility that deep, life-altering communion with Jesus is possible every minute of the day.

Wait—every minute of the day? Seriously? It doesn't make sense, right? We have jobs to do and kids to feed. There's golf on Saturday and hockey practice tomorrow night. No one can live 100 percent fully committed to Christ in every word and action. It's just not possible. But what if it is? What if the measure of true spiritual maturity is not how much we know about the Bible or how many times we go to church? What if it is more about how much we are transformed by the blood of Christ and how much we lean on Him for every decision we make in life? What if the true measure of maturity is more about how much we've been totally transformed by the blood of Jesus? What could we accomplish then?

I used to struggle with the instruction in First Thessalonians 5:17 that says we are to "pray continually." Huh? How is that possible? I've come to realize that having the lifeblood of Jesus means we really do pray constantly, because we are constantly tapped into Him as the source of our spiritual fulfillment. When we are tapped into this source, we can overcome sin. We can pack our bags and head overseas and work with orphans in Uganda. We can humble ourselves enough to stop and seek forgiveness from a spouse who feels neglected.

Of course, the big question is: How? We can agree with the idea of spiritual transfusion as a concept, but how do we make it a reality? It might seem like a nice idea to let Jesus guide our every decision all day long. It might seem fine to live with utter spiritual conviction. Maybe we agree with the core concept that maturity comes through the exchange of our actions, our thoughts, and our ambitions to align with those of our Savior. The hard part is figuring out how to do that in a genuine way. The hard part is living that out even on the days when we feel miserable. Yet when Jesus told us that He is the Bread of Life, it wasn't just a nice idea.

We're supposed to believe that and live as if eating the bread is important. We're supposed to live for the bread. We're supposed to take it seriously.

Lifeblood is a way to examine the actions in our own lives against the truth of our own transfusions. Every decision, every act, every thought—they all have to be fueled by genuine transfusion. We won't ever change in any tangible ways if we don't make daily communion critically important to our lives. We will be stuck with the same old blood. We will sink to the bottom of the lake with spiritual hypothermia, our oxygen depleted and our souls disconnected from the only real life giver.

As tempting as it might be to jump in and start talking about the lifeblood in our churches or workplaces, the act of spiritual transfusion starts with our personal thought lives. It starts with our daily devotions. It can start with nothing more than our own silent, life-changing prayer in the morning, or studying one passage and meditating on what it really means. As we will see, the lifeblood branches out from there into our friendships, marriages, and families, and eventually to a wider circle of influence—our churches, workplaces, and communities.

Lifeblood is highly personal. Did you know that breathing and blood circulation are closely connected? When hypothermia kicks in, blood oxygen levels dip below normal. Breathing becomes difficult. A certain amount of oxygen needs to flow out to the arteries from the heart. Doctors can place a small clip on a person's finger and find out if the oxygen level is normal (about 95 percent or more). If the blood oxygen level is below 90 percent, there's a pretty serious problem. The person has hypothermia. He or she is going to die.

Christians experience a similar condition. We suffer from spiritual hypothermia when we forget to wear a spiritual oxygen mask. We can't breathe in God's Spirit, and we can't exhale His blessing. We're blood sick. The first step in solving that problem is to breathe more deeply. We have to get personal about our spiritual transfusions before we can help anyone else.

Remember that college roommate I mentioned earlier, the one who pulled me from the lake? There's something else you need to know about him. He played a role in my spiritual transformation as well. His name is Doug Traylor. It's been thirty years since I first met him and I've lost contact with him, but Doug made a profound impact on me.

I went to a Bible college in the Twin Cities. In my first semester, I got stuck with a jock who was there to date the ladies and drink beer. I think he was confused about the purpose of Christian education. Fortunately, he left after the Christmas break and my resident assistant shifted me to another room. I felt like he knew I needed the change.

Doug gave me a hearty welcome, and we connected on multiple levels. He even taught me a few things on guitar. This guy also understood lifeblood. I usually woke up to the sound of the crinkling pages of his Bible turning and turning . . . and turning. He studied that book relentlessly and I wondered why he made such a fuss about it. He didn't seem to care that all that crinkling woke me up.

I tried to maintain my distance though. (After all, he was

from Kentucky.) He would disappear for an evening and come back saying he had led a few people to Christ at the mall. Wow, and he bought a new pair of jeans too? The guy was a rock star. Something emanated from Doug. I didn't know it at the time, but it was the Holy Spirit. He had something. I had nothing. We were a match made in heaven. He used to tell me that I was a heathen and going to hell while smiling from ear to ear. I didn't think Christians could be that direct. Maybe it was a sign of immaturity that he could be so brash, but I'm glad he was so confrontational and made me think about all my bad choices.

One day, Doug told me he was heading home for a few days. Maybe he had to feed the chickens. I'm not sure, but I had the room to myself. This created the perfect setting for the Lord to pay me a visit right then and there and bring me to my knees (literally) on the dorm-room carpeting. I prayed my first real prayer ever. It went something like this: "God, I'm really sick of You hounding me. Enough already! Can you please bug someone else? I wish I had never met this guy named Doug. He's a little crazy. And who are You to . . . What? You want what from me? Everything? I have no idea . . . What? My entire life? I don't know what to say. Yes? I'm ready. I want to follow You. I want to be like this Doug guy. Please?"

That was my official prayer of salvation. I still remember the rug burn. I had an open, honest conversation with the God who created me. It wasn't that I wanted knowledge like Doug had or to learn more. I wanted the same *blood* he had. I heard God's voice, not audibly but in a way that was even more real and vibrant. God reached down and put life into my veins.

Early in my Christian life, I felt so connected. I was plugged in. My prayer life had never been so genuine, so spontaneous, so constant. When I became a camp counselor the first summer after I got saved, I led every person in my cabin to Christ every week. I led so many kids in the prayer of salvation that I could almost have done it in my sleep, and I may have done just that a few times. I prayed about dating relationships, finances, the kids at camp, the camp dog—anyone and everything.

Prayer became part of my daily life. I haven't always been perfectly consistent since then. For about ten years in the nineties, when I was climbing the ladder of success in the corporate world, I thought I didn't need a spiritual transfusion anymore. I didn't need to pray that often. I didn't need to spend time in the Word. I lived by *remembrance* of the blood, not through *the blood.* I operated on previous transfusions in my life. (This doesn't work too well when you are still trying to go to church and even trying to share your faith with others.)

This idea of Jesus as our lifeblood starts with just us and Him. Of course, it literally starts when we give our lives to Him. Spiritual transfusion is not possible for those who are not Christians. They have the wrong blood type. Stick the needle in, and nothing happens. Fortunately, for a Christian, receiving a transfusion of Christ's blood is always possible. The Spirit can move at any time and for any purpose, according to Philippians 1. In many ways, we don't even have a choice. God, who started His good work in us, will "carry it on to completion" (Phil. 1:6), which means He will figure out a way to transform our thoughts and actions one way or another. It's all on Him. Don't mess it up!

We have a great need for daily communion. I don't mean the sacrament of Christ's body and blood, although that could help. In the early church, Communion was not on the first Sunday of the month and it didn't take place at 11:45 a.m., right after a condensed sermon. From what I understand, the sacrament was a habitual and common occurrence. What I mean, though, is that we have to have daily communion with God, and the only good example I have of how this works comes from my own life. I have to be real with God every morning and break bread with Him. I have to pray in an intimate and honest way. I have to confess sin and express hurts. I have to open up my spiritual veins and let God do the hard work of transformation in me.

The first time I ever did this in an authentic way was in college. I used to have my devotions at night after everyone else had gone to bed. It was too hard to do them in the morning when I had to rush off to an early morning class. I used to get a big bowl of cereal and sit down with an open Bible. After pouring out the Lucky Charms, I'd pour out my soul. I'd say, "I'm hurting, God. I'm lost. I don't have a plan for what to do after college. I don't even have a plan about what to do tomorrow. I'm not getting good grades. I dropped out of another class. Who do you have picked out for me to marry? Am I even supposed to get married?"

The next day, my roommates would sometimes tell me they had heard me whispering and sobbing. I'd try to explain that I'd been having my devotions, but they thought devotions took five minutes and only involved a brief reading in *Our Daily Bread*, if that. I realized way back then we're supposed to be devoted during our devotions. I viewed those fifteen minutes as a way to commune with God in a vibrant and honest way. I decided I was not going to mess around. Time was short. I wanted my devotions to count.

Fast-forward thirty years, and I still have a "come to Jesus" moment every morning. I hear God speaking to me in ways I can't explain. More importantly, it's a two-way conversation. I ask questions, I talk about challenges, I admit my failings. Then I listen. This is a form of worship. I ask God to help me because I know He can answer me in times of distress.

Just recently, I woke up one morning and asked God to help me with a situation that was out of my control. Some months earlier, my wife and I had decided to move. We put our house on the market and it sold in a week! We did everything we could to choose a new town and new house as wisely as possible. We prayed for guidance. We looked at houses in our price range. We thought about the proximity to a local church, friends and family, and colleges for our kids. At the last minute, we decided to look at one more house in a town a few miles from where we'd initially looked, and we felt God was leading us there.

The place wasn't expensive, but we had to act quickly. We only had thirty days to move. We made an offer and, after some back and forth, agreed to a price. Then came the hard part. I'm a writer, which means I hate crunching numbers. I'd rather crunch on some tree bark. Still, I added up the costs and fees. I asked questions. I made a plan, and it looked legit. The only catch: We had fallen a bit short of the amount of money we needed. So I started praying.

I won't paint a picture of myself as a saint with a halo and a shepherd's staff standing by a peaceful river with a big smile on my face, waiting for God to answer. It's more like I was a shivering peasant on the roadside with a three-day-old beard and my hat tipped down, worried about what was to come next. At least I was by the road waiting, right?

We had prepared and planned for an imminent move, and God had led us to a town that seemed like the place He wanted us to live. (We've since realized He relocated us at just the right time because it led to a new opportunity for me at a Christian college nearby, and my son also became a youth pastor close to our town.) I worked and worked and worked, but the money was not there. All the ducks had lined up, except one that had not been very cooperative. We kept praying for an answer. Checks did start coming in, one after the other, yet I still felt stressed. It wasn't enough.

We needed one last check to arrive the week before we were to move. Again, I'm no saint. I was worried. I didn't feel the presence of God in my life. I didn't feel the lifeblood. Yet I still prayed. I bowed my head one morning that week and asked God to solve the problem.

As most of us know, banks like to see upfront cash when a person takes out a mortgage. As I walked into the foyer of the post office that day, I whispered one last time for resolution. I asked God to reveal Himself to me in a way that only He could.

I'm not into health and wealth, the well-known view that God wants to provide us nice cars and good health at all times. It's a sad statement about Christianity that we try to marginalize God, the Creator of the universe, into a Santa Claus figure who just wants to hand out cash. In such a transaction, who is the god anyway? We confuse the fact that God will bless us because He is a great provider, but we don't quite understand what His blessing means. It is not a BMW or good health. Sometimes it is just a whisper from Him: "I got this."

That day, God provided for me. The money was there at the post office. I had tapped into the lifeblood and leaned on God for understanding, even though it hadn't exactly been a smooth process. Lifeblood is like that. It's a bit messy. It's a continual transformation.

Acts 12 talks about a time when Peter was in jail. James, John's brother, had just been killed by King Herod. There are no details about how Peter was arrested, but his imprisonment must have caused some serious stress for the early church. As he sat in prison waiting for the inevitable, the church started praying for him. Then an angel appeared to Peter and said to him, "Gird yourself" (12:8, NASB).

Wait, what? We don't use the word *gird* anymore. It's never used in a Facebook status update or Instagram post. It means to wrap a belt around your tunic. We don't wear tunics anymore either. But why would the angel bother to tell Peter to get dressed? What's the point? Where was this all leading? As it turned out, it was leading out of the jail.

When we think about it, the instruction to "gird" ourselves reminds us that we have a role to play in our faith, right? We pray, we lean in, we whisper. We ask God to become our redeemer during those times when we really need redemption. We need to do a lot more girding in our personal lives. The challenge in our marriages, the conflict with an angry boss, the temper tantrums the kids are having. We need to be girded for those things. And the only way to gird ourselves is to have a deeper communion with God.

How does that work? Girding is an intentional process. If you're a student, gird yourself before a test. If you're in business, gird yourself before a meeting. Yet we don't really do that. We just rush into things and hope for the best. We trust in our abilities only.

Girding is more than prayer. It's any act of spiritual preparation. It works like this: I'm an avid golfer, but I don't play the kind of golf you think. It's disc golf, a game in which players attempt to throw a disc into a basket instead of drive a ball into a hole. I play at least once a week. I might not be ready for a championship tournament, but I enjoy the exercise and the competition. Sometimes I even win. There's sweet satisfaction in chipping into the basket from fifty feet away. It helps that the sport is entirely free and few people are ever on the course.

A player can take a shot in disc golf in one of two ways. The first is the way most people shoot—no preparation and no strategy. They pick up the disc and let it fly. They don't take the game that seriously because it all seems so trivial (and it's free). A player can decide to stop playing on any hole—which my son does on occasion—and just get something from Dairy Queen. It doesn't really matter that much. It's just disc golf. It's just a game. Then there's the way I shoot. To me, it's more than a game. I take each shot seriously. I plan what I want to do. I plant my feet, practice my swing, and check the wind conditions. I look for obstacles in my way and what the brush looks like around the basket. Then I launch the disc. Whoa! Results.

When I plan the throw and think about the consequences, my shot turns out much better. When I fall back into old habits and don't plan anything, my shot goes awry. The spiritual life is like that. As Christians, we often don't plan our approach. In many ways, because we dive right in, we end up failing. We spin our wheels. We get caught up in the world. We sin.

How can you gird yourself today? How can you ensure you're making decisions and acting under the direction of the Spirit in a vibrant way? It starts and ends with prayer. That communion we have with God is a channel, a conduit. It's meant to give us strength.

In the end, we have to focus on our relationship with Christ—to pray continually, to understand how everything in life flows out of a deeper commitment to Him—so God gets the glory. When we have the lifeblood in us, others will know that there is only one possible reason we can do anything worthwhile.

On the other hand, when we just go through the motions of the Christian life, they see *us*—they see our abilities. They give us the glory, not God. We don't live differently from others; we just convince people that we have a spiritual bent and talk like committed Christians. We are good at mimicking the way we're supposed to live, yet we lack depth. When hard times come, the spiritual blood in our veins is so thin that we collapse in a heap. Our energy runs out because we are doing all that spiritual stuff in our own power and ability.

Want more power? First make a personal commitment to commune with God—put the oxygen mask on yourself. Then the lifeblood in you will touch a wide circle of influence: your friends, your marriage, your church, and beyond.

PRINCIPLES FOR THE LIFEBLOOD IN OUR PERSONAL LIVES

Our intimate relationship with Christ is by far the most important one if we are interested in lifeblood living. That's why it's crucial to take some time to consider the following eight principles that will guide us to a deeper "blood level" faith, a lifeblood faith.

1. Listen up. God is speaking to us. Did you read that correctly? Yes, you did. The God of the universe has something to tell each of us daily through His Word and the voice of the Holy Spirit. When God talks, it's a good idea for us to listen. Lifeblood means eternity has invaded our hearts, so we need to make sure we pay attention.

2. Invest often. This listening is an investment. We must tune

our ears to it. Tune our souls to it. When we decide to pursue intimacy with God, we need to make an investment and make it a routine. A sure sign that we want to have lifeblood in our veins is that we become consistent about time with God.

3. Go deep. Intimacy and depth are closely related. When we need a blood test, we don't just get a pin prick. The doctor draws a sample to go deep. To reveal what we need to reveal to God, we must confess our sin. We also have to be ready to expose our deepest longings and hurts.

4. Enjoy God's presence. Once we are at a place of deep surrender, it's okay to bask in the glow of the Savior's love. We can let it overwhelm and consume us. We should live in the moment with the Spirit.

5. Bring the hurt. I mentioned how we should share our hurts. God is listening. Part of the process of going deeper in our communion with Christ is being honest and real, exposing what needs to be exposed, letting His love cover our hurts.

6. Open up. We need to be real about our ambitions, our goals, our plans. We must let God direct them and be careful to avoid letting our plans interfere with His mission.

7. Offer praise. We should thank the Savior for invading our bloodstream, and transforming who we are and what we will become by His grace. We need to praise Him for the transformative work He is doing in us.

8. Decide to change. We must let the lifeblood flow. Get personal. Pray continually. When we do, we will become ready to move on to other relationships in life, including our close friends, spouses, and kids.

STUDY QUESTIONS

1. Where have you seen the lifeblood in your personal relationship to Christ?
2. What's one change you could make to encourage more lifeblood daily?
3. Was there a time when lifeblood was thin in your life? How did you make changes?
4. What are the most important ways to encourage the lifeblood flow?
5. What's the most recent example of the Holy Spirit guiding you?
6. Is it easy to have lifeblood in your veins? Why or why not?

2

THE LIFEBLOOD IN OUR FRIENDSHIPS

Jian Zhou had an interesting way of throwing a Frisbee. I was visiting Hamline University in the fall of 1985, trying to round up other students to play Ultimate Frisbee with me and my friends. The game was popular in the eighties, died out for a while in the nineties, and has come back with a vengeance in the past few years—although it's not quite an Olympic sport (yet).

It's a bit like football. Players have to work as a team. One player throws the disc as a kickoff, then the other team keeps throwing to its players (each one gets three steps after a catch) to reach the end zone. As a technique for evangelistic outreach, the game is a perfect match for college students. The rules are simple and anyone can play—male or female, athletes and nonathletes alike.

Jian was sitting by the field, reading a book and watching me and my friends pick teams as we joked around and made fun of each other. I walked over to him and motioned back toward the team.

"You want to join us?" I asked in a way that said, "No pressure."

"No, no play," he said, smiling. His book suddenly became more interesting to him.

"You sure? I can teach you how to throw."

He stared at me with a blank expression.

"Okay," he said after a long pause, "I will. Fine."

I wondered if he was being polite. He was a Chinese student, a sophomore, and he may have thought it would be rude to tell me no. We made an odd pair walking onto the field. I'm the size of a football player, and he looked like he was ready for a marathon.

"Okay, so you throw with an arc, like this," I said, demonstrating the standard forearm toss. He didn't quite understand, but we put him on a team anyway. He had an unusual throwing style. He'd hold his index finger on the edge of the Frisbee, apply pressure, and then fling it forward. Somehow he managed to make a few throws worthy of high fives.

"We're going to grab some food after the game. Do you want to join us?" my friend Paul asked Jian. Our team didn't look like an imposing bunch, about eight American guys and a couple of women who had opted out of the game, laughing and joking around. Jian didn't know we were there as part of the Navigators group from Northwestern College (now the University of Northwestern) doing outreach, making initial contacts with students, and asking spiritual questions. This was around the time the term *friendship evangelism* became popular among Christians who were reacting to the pressure tactics so common before then. We knew enough about outreach to know that no one would probably want to join a Bible study right away. We had decided to play Ultimate Frisbee and invite people to play, then develop relationships.

Jian walked with us to a pizza place close to campus and chatted about classes and studying. Everyone enjoyed each other's company, but Jian looked a little uncomfortable. I asked if he needed to go study and he took the opportunity to say goodbye. I asked him if we could chat again sometime and he looked a little confused. He nodded and motioned toward his dorm room as if to say he needed to go.

I was a little clueless about Asian customs. It's possible he had felt like he'd had to agree to play Ultimate Frisbee and had felt obligated to join us for pizza as well. My kids all went to a Christian high school attended by quite a few South Korean students, so as an adult, I later found out about how important it is for Asians to show respect and honor to others. At the time, I wasn't thinking about it because I just bumbled along, unaware of his feelings.

About a week later, our group went back to Hamline. We often went door to door and asked students in the dorm, "Do you think the Bible is true or just another book?" or "What are your favorite parts of the Bible?" They were all open-ended questions, no pressure, but still a few students slammed the door on us. But after knocking on almost every door on one floor, we usually ended up getting a handful of students to say yes. This time no one seemed interested, so we kept knocking. We came to the end of a floor and knocked on one last door. It was Jian's room. When he opened the door, he seemed a bit startled.

I was with my friend Paul again and another guy named Ken, and we all remembered the Chinese student who threw the Frisbee with his index finger.

"Hey, Jian! Remember us?" Paul asked excitedly. He was the outgoing type and immediately started chatting with Jian. I could tell Jian wasn't sure why we were there.

"Good to see you again," I said, glancing at my two friends to indicate that it was time to go and relieve the awkward silence. After a few minutes, we left for the day and talked about how Jian seemed uncomfortable with us. We decided not to push things with him.

A few weeks went by and we visited other local college campuses, including the University of Minnesota, close to downtown Minneapolis, and Macalester College in Saint Paul. That fall, we tried to start several more Bible studies and even visited a mosque a few times, chatting with some Muslim students and asking them about their faith.

As a sophomore myself, I had become a committed Christian only the year before—in a dorm room, all by myself. New to the faith and full of excitement, I had visions of heading out to some foreign country as a missionary and sharing Christ with people on every street corner. Sharing Christ had become the new normal for me, even with total strangers on the bus, to paraphrase the song by Joan Osborne that you probably have never heard before.

I did not forgot about Jian. I knew he was adjusting to life as a foreigner in the United States, and the program for Chinese students at Hamline was relatively new. I had no plan or strategy other than spending more time there. God was speaking to me quite clearly in those days. I wasn't using the word *lifeblood* then and I wasn't talking too much about the Holy Spirit indwelling every fiber of my being, but I was living it out in real time.

Every morning, I read my Bible for at least an hour, usually before dawn over a bowl of Cheerios. I memorized verses using index cards, a technique every person who has any connection with the Navigators knows all about. I prayed for any college students I might meet that day. Intimacy with Christ ran through my soul like a river, and I lived it in a way I'd never experienced before. It was all new to me.

One day, I went by myself to Hamline and started knocking on doors. A few guys agreed to meet in the lounge and talk about the Bible. I suspected one of them had a hidden agenda—he wanted to talk me out of believing that the Bible had anything relevant to say.

We scheduled the study for later that day; and when the time arrived, a few students showed up. To my surprise, one of them was Jian. He came with his roommate, who I later found out had been witnessing to him as well. Maybe his roommate had physically dragged him out of their dorm room or bribed him to come somehow.

"Jian, how are you doing? I haven't seen you in a while!" I said, surprised.

You may notice a theme here: Jian looked uncomfortable again and a little shocked to see me. Once again, I was oblivious to Asian cultural norms. Maybe our meeting was providential, but I'm sure Jian thought I was a wacko. "How are your classes going?" I asked.

We bantered back and forth, but we eventually read a passage in John 1 about how the Word became flesh. I can imagine now how Jian may have been confused by those verses; and to be honest, they do sound strange even now. What is the Word? Who is the Word? How did it become flesh? And why? Because these verses are so unusual, we knew they were a good place to start in terms of talking about our faith. Many of our conversations back then focused on the nature of God and His purpose. We knew some of the guys were sleeping with their girlfriends. Many had never heard about Jesus.

Jian never did engage with our discussion, but something else clicked for him. He was interested in American culture. Why else had he come to America? He liked hearing about our customs, and he liked hanging out.

We talked for a bit after the study and agreed to meet again. This time, it was probably not related to his desire to show respect but more of an interest in hearing about my life in America. I was interested in talking to him and he was interested in learning. Our conversation had no spiritual underpinnings at all, even if everything seemed to be pointing in that direction. In other words, the Spirit was moving but this "movement" had more to do with a conversation about Ultimate Frisbee, eating pizza, and maybe going to a concert around campus. Yet it was strange how God was using me even then, despite my cluelessness.

Eventually, we became friends and started getting together once a week. One night, after we had talked for a few hours, Jian suggested we get some snacks at a local convenience store. I had a 1976 Monte Carlo, a big car with a big engine, and he was not used to American drivers. It was around November and there was snow on the ground.

"Watch out!" he yelled when I spun out around a corner. He freaked out about the snow, the muscle car, and this strange American friend who liked Frisbee and pizza.

When we arrived back on campus, I mentioned to Jian that I was a Christian. We had been friends for at least six or eight weeks by this time. I knew Christmas was coming up soon, and

I asked if he would like to join me for my extended family's holiday get-together. He agreed, perhaps against his better judgment (since he had just seen me drive).

Seeing around thirty or forty people celebrating Christmas on a farm in Maple Plain, Minnesota must have seemed a bit surreal to him. My grandmother made an extra effort to talk to Jian. She asked about his culture and how he liked Hamline. In fact, all my relatives welcomed him with open arms. He even sang a Christmas solo in broken English and horribly out of tune (both the guitar he played and his voice). I loved it—he was connecting with everyone. On the way home after the meal, with my sister in the car, we talked about American customs. Jian barely noticed we had been driving in a blizzard all the way home. He was captivated by this American family and how we all seemed to enjoy each other's company.

Christmas break came and went, and we buckled down for the second semester. I met with Jian every week. I mentioned my faith a few times, but we mostly talked about America. His favorite topic? My childhood stories about growing up in the suburbs. He was interested in what American life was like. We also talked about the Christmas we spent together, played the guitar, and sang a few worship songs. Somehow it made a big impact on him.

My friends in the Navigators knew I was becoming friends with Jian but had not yet shared the gospel with him. In my own prayer time, God sometimes whispered to me, "Not yet." As I drew closer and closer into a deep relationship with Christ, I was becoming more attuned to the Spirit leading me. It's amazing to think that this spiritual revitalization was manifesting itself in me so quickly and in ways that now seem so obvious.

One of the keys to my friendship with Jian was that I applied no pressure to him. I had no ulterior motives. I did have spiritual motives—I wanted Jian to discover the same deep spiritual transformation that was fresh on my mind (and in my soul), and everything about our becoming friends was focused on that goal. I didn't want my new friend to go back to China and never hear about Jesus or how He had changed my life.

And then the door opened.

One night Jian wanted to play guitar and learn some new songs, but he kept asking about my faith. It seemed strange to me. He had never asked about Christianity before.

"When you say 'Jesus is my Savior,' what do you mean?" he asked.

It was an odd question. I had never shared the gospel with him. I had never mentioned anything about Jesus being our Savior. I asked him where he had heard that phrase and he said he had read about it in a book his roommate had given him over the break.

"Tell me if this is right," he said. "In my religion, we believe you must swim across a vast ocean. If you make any mistakes, you will sink to the bottom. Only a few make it all the way across, but it is very hard. I think what you are saying is that I can swim on the back of Jesus, and He will save me. He will swim to the other side of the ocean, and I will be saved."

I couldn't believe it. He was correct. I had never heard an analogy like that, but it made perfect sense. More importantly, it made perfect sense to Jian.

"Jian, do you want to give your life to Christ?"

He nodded and bowed his head. It was as though the Holy Spirit had opened his eyes. I was so surprised by his analogy and his questions about spiritual things that I led him in the prayer of salvation in the only way I could remember, saying a phrase and having him repeat it. Maybe that is too old-school for modern sensibilities, maybe it is not elaborate enough. For Jian, it was as though the clouds opened and he could finally see the sun.

For many more weeks, we met and studied the Bible. He had so many questions! He asked about how he would continue to live for Christ in his home country and the many challenges of being a Christian in China when there were so few official churches. We talked about how he would need to keep studying the Bible, and I gave him a new copy. I also gave him several Bible studies and books to take home with him.

Late that semester, we met one last time. He had spent his sophomore year at Hamline and he was preparing to fly back to China. We prayed in a cafeteria close to his dorm room and the tears came. We hugged and I told him I would see him again.

I walked back to my car. It was raining, and in the darkness I could barely find my parking spot a block up the street. I unlocked the door, threw my jacket inside, and looked back. Jian was still standing at the entrance to the cafeteria, watching me.

What happened way back then? What had started with a game of Ultimate Frisbee ended with a Chinese student finding Christ for the first time.

Jian and I kept in touch through letters. A few years after we had said goodbye, one of Jian's letters was strangely vague. It was around the spring of 1989. I was married, had a new baby, and was living with my family in a small apartment. I knew Jian was living in Beijing because of the return postmark and how he had written about being a student there. The letter said, "I am working in carpet factory and you know why." That was a strange thing to write because I didn't know why. If Jian was at Beijing University, why was he working at a carpet factory? It was an unusual thing for him to tell me.

Maybe he was trying to say something about the Chinese government. I'm not sure, and I never found out. A few weeks later, the Tiananmen Square protests erupted, and many university students were involved. I never received another letter from him.

Here's what I do know.

Jian had embraced his new life in Christ. A cynic might say he accepted something American, a new way of thinking, a set of ideas. I saw a life changed. He acted differently, he prayed differently. When we met those last few times, he stopped asking so many questions and started sharing what he had learned using his new Bible in his own Bible study. He started talking about the danger he might face in China living as a new Christian.

God had moved in his heart and Jian started a journey of total surrender. The lifeblood flowed into our friendship for the first time. I'll never forget the experience.

In many ways, our friendships are the next steps in our journey to pursue lifeblood after our own personal relationship with Christ, especially with other Christians who are committed to mentoring and discipleship. Why is that? For starters, even though marriage is the closest relationship some of us will pursue in our lives, not everyone is married. Also, friendship is modeled in Scripture. Judging from the examples we have in the Gospels, Jesus wasn't just in a business relationship with His disciples so He could strategically advance the church on earth. The disciples were His close friends. He loved them. He cooked them breakfast on at least one occasion.

Ed Phelps, founder of Pocket Awareness, says, "A people focused definition of friendship is 'a state of mutual trust and support between persons.'"[1] We lean on our friends to hold us up. We trust them with our emotions, giving them permission to hold us accountable. Trust is an act of permission. We agree to let another person speak wisdom into our lives. It's also a journey, of course. We don't trust our friends completely when we first meet them. Trust is a gradual development.

We can read about how this spiritual journey of lifeblood in friendship works in Second Peter 1.

> His divine power has granted to us all things that pertain to life and godliness, through the knowledge of him who called us to his own glory and excellence, by which he has granted to us his precious and very great promises, so that through them you may become partakers of the divine nature, having escaped from the corruption that is in the world because of sinful desire. (1:3–4, ESV)

That's God's part. The passage continues with our responsibility.

> For this very reason, make every effort to supplement your faith with virtue, and virtue with knowledge, and knowledge with self-control, and self-control with steadfastness, and steadfastness with godliness, and godliness with brotherly affection, and brotherly affection with love. For if these qualities are yours and are increasing, they keep you from being ineffective or unfruitful in the knowledge of our Lord

> Jesus Christ. For whoever lacks these qualities is so nearsighted that he is blind, having forgotten that he was cleansed from his former sins. (2 Pet. 1:5–9, ESV)

You may already know about adding to your faith in this passage, but these verses contain an idea that might be easy to overlook. Second Peter 1:3 talks about the lifeblood—it is only by God's "divine power" that we can add anything at all to our faith. It is in the lifeblood that we can find our lives and build trust in our friendships.

As with any biblical passage, the order of these verses is important. We can't increase our own faith—we can't add brotherly kindness or self-control to it—without the power of the cross. Why do people still try to construct their own form of religion? Because it's easier than letting God work through us. Because it's a great way to get a compliment. Because it's the safe method. Because it's how we think as humans. We tend to build things we can control and manage, things we can summarize and understand. We like to make sure we maintain a degree of decorum with religion.

Friendship needs a root grounded in and formed by lifeblood. Think about it this way: A casual friendship is like buying a plant at the garden store. It already has leaves; it's already sprouted. A deeper friendship, one that lasts for years, is more like a seed we plant in the ground. We water it, we cut away the weeds, and eventually we see growth. No shortcuts. There is no question as to why or how such a friendship grows. We cultivate it.

That's what happened with my friend Jian. He didn't respond to a three-point sermon. He wasn't impressed by my exceptional Frisbee talents. (I must admit that I was by far the most accomplished player on the field that day when we first met.) What he really saw was daily devotion—a condition of the soul, like a river flowing underground and out of sight. He watched me cultivating our friendship. This kind of devotion to a person is due to the lifeblood, so it was not about me. I didn't get the credit. We can buy a plant at the store; but when we grow a seed, we see the miracle of growth.

We can't always see the lifeblood, and our friends may not either. It's a miracle in many ways, something only God can cultivate. I've become a gardener over the years and I have several indoor plants in my office. They require quite a bit of work. To pollinate the fruit plants, I have to use my hands since no bees are flying around my office. I have to add water once a week. The wonderful thing about growing these plants is that I see each step in the process, and I realize that I merely play a role in how the plants grow and develop.

People don't always see our true nature, especially at the beginning of a friendship. Most people are drawn to the things of the world—a winning personality or a nice hairstyle. We're flesh driven. Any of us, spiritual or not, can play a Chris Tomlin song in the car when we drive with a friend. There is no spiritual gate check at church, no Christian security guard monitoring people for an insincere heart. We sometimes fake our way through the Christian life and some of us present a loftier image of ourselves than is warranted.

We also see only what we want to at times. True spiritual devotion, the kind that is in our blood, runs deep and isn't flashy. It takes time to develop. In a church setting, where we might find the most opportunity for friendships, no award is given for having the lifeblood in us. In many ways, only God knows if we have developed an inner life meant only for His glory. How could a pastor hand out such an award anyway? Instead, we hand out awards for memorizing the most verses in a kids' club. (I'm happy to see kids memorize verses; I'm even happier when they apply what they've learned to real life.)

I could have checked those weekly meetings with Jian off my list, since I'd done what the Navigators materials I used to collect at seminars and retreats said to do. I could have checked evangelism off my list. But the hard way was building a friendship over many weeks.

Friendship must be genuine. We might try to show a friend that we are intellectual or can tell funny jokes, but every friendship grows closer or grows apart, one way or another. A strong friendship is enriched and solidifies over time. The surface-level nature of a casual friendship means it can easily split apart. Without a spiritual root causing friendship to grow, without the water needed to spur us into maturity in a way that is spiritually sound, we go with whatever works in many relationships. Our friendships stay shallow, thin, and a bit empty.

In any friendship it's important to become intentional. With friends who are not Christians, the lifeblood in us reveals true devotion to them. With friends who are Christians, the bond of lifeblood leads us to great depths of understanding and commitment, a deep devotion to one another. This is also true in marriage, and with siblings and parents. We must reveal even the deep parts of who we are in the relationship, our inner thoughts and feelings. The lifeblood in any friendship must flow in both directions, united and intertwined in a way that only the Holy Spirit can codify (that is, turn into something profound).

Zach Williams shows how this works in his song "To the Table (from his album Chain Breaker)."

Hear the voice of love that's calling;
There's a chair that waits for you
And a Friend who understands
Everything you're going through.

But you keep standing at a distance
In the shadow of your shame;
There's a light of hope that's shining;
Won't you come and take your place

And bring it all to the table?
There's nothing He ain't seen before.
For all your fear, all your sorrow and your sadness,
There's a Savior, and He calls,
"Bring it all to the table."

He can see the weight you carry,
The fears that hold your heart;
But through the cross you've been forgiven;
You're accepted as you are.

So bring it all to the table;
There's nothing He ain't seen before.
For all your trials, all your worries and your burdens,
There's a Savior, and He calls,
"Bring it all to the table."

Bring it all,
You can bring it all.

And come on in, take your place;
There's no one who's turned away.

All you sinners, all you saints,
Come right in and find your grace

And bring it all to the table.
There's nothing He ain't seen before.
For all your sin, all your sorrow and your sadness,
There's a Savior, and He calls,
"Bring it all to the table."

Did you catch that? It has to be *all.* All of who we are. All of who we are meant to be. A true friendship with lifeblood flowing through it should be the best relationship we could ever imagine apart from marriage. No lies, no shadows, no illusions. While we don't have to reveal every last detail about ourselves, our openness and honesty about our dreams, failings, and true motivations strengthen a relationship. When we clearly present the inner core of who we are, we change and grow in our friendships and as people.

I experienced this when I started meeting with a new friend, first to get to know him better and then as an accountability partner. We first met in the hallway at church.

"My name is Tim," he said as he shook my hand. I noticed something different about him right away. He exuded confidence but not pride. He seemed friendly enough but not overly familiar. I also sensed a spiritual depth about him.

We didn't become friends right away. We're quite different. I'm a writer and he works in sales. He's a bit older than I am, although our kids are about the same ages. He's stocky and Norwegian, and I'm tall and—Norwegian (and Swedish). Our shared heritage meant we had one common interest: drinking coffee.

One day, I bumped into him again in the hallway at church. We started talking, and I told him about a big life decision I had to make. I had just returned from Texas, where I had interviewed for a new job, and I asked him for advice. That sparked an idea about mentoring and accountability.

We decided to meet regularly. Our discussions were wide open, a free-form dialogue that could consume two hours and a few carafes of coffee by the time we were done. Predestination? Check. Justification by faith? Done. We didn't always agree on the topics, and the only thing we ever got heated about was the stale coffee (and maybe the subject of eternal salvation), but we left all the huffing and puffing for the gym. We talked about our relationships with our wives and children, we discussed how to live more radical lives for Jesus, we planted seeds that germinated and grew over time. The lifeblood concept likely came out of one of these discussions.

Tim and I talked a lot about church. What is it? Why does it exist? Who should be on the worship team and why? Should it let people smoke in the parking lot? I won most of the debates—I can say that now since I'm writing this book and he isn't. In the end though, he won the war, because it was usually my pride that was left on the floor, ready to be mopped up.

We read *Radical* (by David Platt) together. Someone probably could have dropped a piano on my foot at the time and it would have made less of an impact on me than that book did. *Radical* is life-altering. It reiterates what we already know from the Bible; but if a person took it seriously, he or she might end up adopting kids or becoming a missionary. It has that effect on people. My friend Tim ended up moving across Minnesota to help start a church, where he is now an executive pastor. I'm living my own "radical." You're reading it. Several decisions I've made since then have also been radical, including one to take a part-time role at a Christian college in late 2016.

The point is, a friendship with lifeblood leads to real change and real growth. Tim and I inhaled our breakfasts and shared the insights we were uncovering. I'll always remember how many times we confided in each other and shared some of our biggest dreams.

The story in First Samuel 18:1 describes a close friendship like that and refers to "knitting" (ESV). I love it when the Bible uses these kinds of words. Knitting comes up again in Psalm 139:13 (the verse about being knit together in the womb). In the New Testament, Colossians 2:2 talks about a close communion in church and how everyone was "knit together" (ESV).

When we think about lifeblood, we can think about how knitting works. (Full disclosure here: I've never even knitted a pair of socks, but I've seen people do it.) When knitting, a person weaves yarn together in a series of loops to create a whole item. In our devotion to Christ, we create a similar bond with Him that forms our identity. We are alive in Christ, and Christ is alive in us. We are alive in the Spirit, and the Spirit is alive in us. We are changed forever.

The forever friendship between King David and Jonathan, son of King Saul, had an inextricable bond, like a piece of yarn that has been twisted into a new creation. First Samuel 18:1 describes how Jonathan was "knit to the soul" of David (ESV) and how they were "one in spirit" (NIV). We might say that they were best buds in the vernacular of today, hanging out as much as possible.

I can imagine these two in battle, one watching the other's

flank. Back to back, they battled the Philistine armies until they routed them. Talk about doing life together as Christians. These two likely knew each other's combat maneuvers and were locked in perfect step. But they needed each other even when they were not on the battlefield. Because, to be honest, times were a little difficult.

In First Samuel 18:11, we find that Jonathan's father, King Saul, wanted to pin David to the wall with a spear. (We read a lot of verses in this passage about Saul throwing spears at people.) Yet in verse 14, we find out that David had "success in all his undertakings" (ESV). King Saul was jealous about that for sure and seemed to have many other issues with the future leader of Israel.

Jonathan picked his side. In First Samuel 23:16, we read that Jonathan chose to help David in battle. We can picture him rushing off, forgetting his armor, and leaving a hot bowl of soup on the table. Jonathan "strengthened [David's] hand in God" (ESV), which sounds like an act of pure friendship—a sacrifice and a blessing all rolled into one. There's no question that this was a friendship built on loyalty and kinship, and the bond was not light or fragile.

What we do and what comes out of our mouths emanate from either a transfused soul or a nontransfused soul. And receiving a blood transfusion from Christ is a daily process. Sin can corrupt our inner lives like a disease flowing through our veins—almost undetectable unless we submit to a spiritual blood test. There's a quick mention of this in First Samuel 24:13 that references an ancient proverb: "Out of the wicked comes wickedness" (ESV). When we lean on our own understanding, we typically fail. When we lean on the sure hand of the Savior by His lifeblood, we trust that He will carry us, assist us, even win our battles for us. We don't expect the outcome to be exactly what we want, but we expect the outcome to honor God. Friendship requires the same dependencies.

When Jonathan died, David referred to his friend one last time. In Second Samuel 1:26, he said that this friend had showed love to him more than any woman had in his life. Say what you want about how marital relationships worked back then, but it's clear that David and Jonathan were close. They shared every fear, every success, every life goal with each other. They didn't hold back.

You might have one or two friends like that. Most of us have friendships not quite as close. To be blood brothers or blood sisters means to become mutual mentors, to have an understanding and perspective about each other that is entirely unique. It means a devotion to each other—if the two are in the same room, they will find each other just to talk.

My wife has a friend like that. When they get together to walk at the mall or share a sandwich, they commune at a deep level. It's more than picking up where the last conversation left off. It's like they are breaking bread together. Their hopes and fears, their joys and sorrows—it's all there right on the table at Pizza Hut. There's no hiding behind a veneer. I've experienced that as well.

My friend Tim had a way of looking me straight in the eyes and delivering sound advice. At least it seemed like sound advice. (Maybe I should have tried to analyze it more.) We can't grow deep in any friendship unless we are honest and real. We must present an image of ourselves that is as accurate as possible and to do that, we need lifeblood. Any other presentation to a friend is a pure sham, like a bad concert with bad lighting, attended by people who don't really want to be there. We must be willing to ask each other difficult, thought-provoking, penetrating questions.

"Do you think that will help your relationship with your daughter or hurt it?" Tim would ask me.

Good question. I have no idea. Let me get back to you about that one.

"Are you being the husband your wife needs you to be?" he'd ask.

Er, not sure. Can I mull that over for a few weeks and then answer?

Any good friendship will thrive in difficult circumstances because the lifeblood in our relationships suddenly provides the power and momentum to resolve conflicts. Wing it and go with a more shallow image of our inner lives, and we will end up suffering. When we present a false image to a friend, the bond we form with that person is weak. With lifeblood we have a strong bond—a friendship deep enough and strong enough to last.

Many of us choose to keep our friendships shallow for a reason. Honestly, they are easier to manage that way. How can we go deep when there are so many shows to spend our time watching on Netflix? Why engage in conversation when we can just send a text? We choose to be shallow because depth requires honesty, conviction, devotion, and time. Yet the byproduct of keeping every friend at a safe distance is that we don't change. The expression *at arm's length* means to refrain from having any intimacy. A correlating term in the business world is the *arm's length principle*, which means that everyone agrees to keep things civil and fair.

In college, a friend used to tell me, "Everything in moderation." I used to think that was a Chinese proverb, but a few verses support the view. One is First Corinthians 9:25. It says athletes should keep everything in control (or moderation). It's talking about being steady, about not destroying our bodies with excessiveness. But we misuse the verse. When we say "everything in moderation," we try to apply it to everything, including friendships.

In many cases, the opposite makes more sense. Instead of doing *everything* in moderation, we should do some things with radical abandonment. Some things should be moderated; some should be a little reckless. In Revelation 3:16, we find a warning that we need to be either hot or cold. No moderation there! We should be a bit reckless in our devotion to Christ and to one another.

What does a friendship that's a bit reckless look like? Tim was selling his retail store during the time when I met him. I didn't know him well, but I decided to help him close his business. I helped with the cleaning, which didn't take much time, maybe a Saturday afternoon. I asked a lot of questions about his plans. I invested in at least attempting to understand what he was going through.

Say a friend is having trouble in his marriage. He shows up at your door one night. Do you brush him off? Not at all. The lifeblood of pure intimacy with Christ means that we would not turn a friend away, even if our friend shows up at three in the morning unannounced. I'm not saying we should become doormats, that we should drop what we're doing to help any friend at any time. But living with a Spirit-directed mentality means that we will know when to act and when not to act; we will listen with ears attuned to spiritual things. We won't be lost in a sea of indecision, wholly dependent on our own talents and decision making.

Will you commit to being that friend who lets the lifeblood dictate how much you expose your deepest hurts and how far you are willing to take the friendship? Will you be the Jonathan to a David? Will you become knit together in a close friendship?

PRINCIPLES FOR THE LIFEBLOOD IN OUR FRIENDSHIPS

To help grow the lifeblood in friendship, consider these five rules of engagement.

1. Share the deep hurts with no fear. No one likes to be around people who constantly gripe or complain. But there's a difference between revealing hurts and being negative. When we share honestly and openly with a friend, we're inviting that person to make a difference in our lives, to be an active observer, to critique and assist us. We should make our sharing about seeking an honest outcome.

2. Take your time. I'm guilty of being too impatient in friendships, wanting them to evolve quickly. The truth is, a great friendship takes time because we're human. We don't always trust easily. It's important to let those deeper thoughts, those lifeblood moments, germinate and develop. Like seeds in a garden, watering and cultivating friendships will cause them to grow into maturity.

3. Remember that friendships are seasonal. Most of my deepest friendships lasted for many years, even decades. Yet situations do change. We need to see our friendships as deep and rewarding. Make the most of them, but know that there are times when we might have to let go of a deep friendship and start looking for other relationships to develop. We should be that person who is always open to making new friends.

4. Not all friendships will have lifeblood. I've spent many pages on the idea of lifeblood flowing in our personal lives.

Lifeblood can also happen in friendships. Will it happen with everyone we meet? Not at all. The gas station attendant up the block from our house might not be ready to tell us his life story. We should be selective and intentional in developing friendships with people who are ready to have a depth of unity.

5. Be ready to invest. Not only do friendships take time, they also require an investment. We might have to break off some other commitments. (The community basketball league can find another power forward. The community park program can find a new volunteer to water the plants.) A deep friendship might even require that we invest money—say, paying the bill when we eat out. For lifeblood in friendship to develop, it's going to take some sacrifice on our part.

STUDY QUESTIONS

1. Do you have a lifeblood friend? Why or why not?
2. What are some signs of lifeblood in friendship?
3. How do you need to change as a friend so that the Holy Spirit guides your friendships?
4. What impedes lifeblood in friendship?
5. How is lifeblood in friendship different from your personal relationship with Christ?
6. Why is lifeblood in friendship even important?

3

THE LIFEBLOOD IN OUR CHURCHES

Kimball, Minnesota is a town you'll likely never visit. Located about an hour west of the Twin Cities, it is not listed in any of the travel brochures for the state, and you won't find it in one of those glossy Fodor's travel books.

Kimball is surrounded by farm fields. And cows. And more cows. There's also a bar on the edge of town, with Chevy and Ford pickups lined up outside it in a nice neat row. This peaceful villa has no Walmart, no shopping mall—just a bar, some trees, and open fields.

I've driven through the town countless times. Blink and you may miss it. I used to drive my family through Kimball on our way to vacation at a state park. You could say I've never "been" to Kimball because I've never stopped there for gas, I've never talked to anyone who lived there, and I've completely ignored everything about it.

One winter evening, my wife and I drove to that same state park, hoping to hang out together and do a prayer walk. As we approached Kimball, I happened to look up to my right. In the distance, maybe a few miles away, I saw a mountain.

In Kimball, Minnesota.

That people use for skiing.

It's called Powder Ridge and it's awesome.

Now, if you live in Denver or near any real mountains, don't laugh. I know Powder Ridge is basically a big hill. But with a big hill in Minnesota, there is only one thing to do: Put a ski resort on it. This one has multiple ski slopes and jumps. At night, the hill looks like a glowing beacon of hope. (One hope is that you won't realize it's a hill instead of a mountain.) The snowy peak, the lights along the slope, the sudden surprise—it was quite an epiphany for me. I had never realized that there was a skiing hill in Kimball.

I mentioned the hill to my wife as we drove past.

"It's been there a few decades," she said, bursting my epiphany with a poof. A few decades? Really? And I had never looked up and noticed it until now? As Donald Trump would say, "It's huge!" The hill can be seen for miles, but I had never looked in that direction.

I wonder if we're missing it in modern church as well. The church can be a bastion of hope and forgiveness, but we sometimes talk more about the rules, the free barbecue next Saturday, and the elder board report from the last youth group fund-raiser.

When I read Second Corinthians 4:6, I see something much more profound: "God, who said, 'Light shall shine out of darkness,' is the One who has shone in our hearts to give the Light of the knowledge of the glory of God in the face of Christ" (NASB).

We're human, and church is run by people who are not always in perfect step with the Holy Spirit. (Few of us can claim to be the apostle Paul in the flesh, but good luck trying.) Our every decision and act should be tuned toward heaven. While some activities in church will be mundane—someone needs to stack the chairs after the men's breakfast—an unquenched passion should drive us. It should even define us.

In a message I heard at Grace Church of Roseville, Minnesota, where my daughter attends, Pastor Jason Stonehouse mentioned this idea. He said we must tune in to what God is doing. This takes work. It's not easy. When we keep doing the same thing over and over, obeying the rules and following a dictum, we miss the deeper truths. We miss the depths of insight found only in the lifeblood. Leading the church becomes nothing more than a boring ritual of buying crackers and grape juice at Walmart for Communion on Sunday, or trying to entertain people so they come back next Sunday. It's far from the earth-shattering communion God wants with us.

I was once on a hike with my youngest daughter, Katie. We were walking on a trail close to our house and we got a little lost. "No need to worry," I told her. I knew the trails. It was a simple matter of finding a different route back to the car. I'm a techie, so I had an app on my phone guiding us in the right direction. I wasn't ready to panic. We were having fun.

Then we came to a new trail. Well, it was new to me anyway. I'm sure the park rangers were not surprised by its existence, and it had likely been there for a decade. (Maybe these same park rangers also knew about the ski hill in Kimball, I'm not sure.) The funny thing is, this trail happens to arc around a hidden lake, one that has a spectacular view—of our own neighborhood. When you climb up a little embankment, you can see our house off in the distance.

Who knew? Not me. I was too busy sticking to the trails I knew, the ones that wind around too close to a beaver dam and some pricklies that get stuck on your socks and shoelaces. I didn't know there was a better way.

I miss things like this all the time. Once, on a business trip in Austin, Texas, I drove down the wrong street and noticed a bike trail along the river close to downtown. I had visited this area many times, but I had never taken that street or noticed the trail. I also didn't know that this bike trail was considered one of the best in the entire state. It has bridges that are meant only for bikes. The bridges don't cross the river but just wind out over the water in curvy patterns because, well, this is Texas. They do things like that. You can bike for miles on perfectly paved trails, which is exactly what I ended up doing the next day.

It's wonderful to find these hidden treasures. A fruit stand by your place of work, tucked behind a building. A coffee shop, known for its fine blend, located in a hotel you've visited countless times but had never noticed before. I've been an avid basketball fan my whole life; but I started watching the Golden State Warriors only a year ago, never realizing that Stephen Curry is one of the most exciting players on any professional sports team. I mentioned earlier my love and passion for disc golf. The game existed when I was a teenager. I just didn't know about it.

In the western part of Minnesota, where we used to live, there is a place called Orwell Dam. Few people knew about it. Every spring, I took my son and son-in-law there, and we'd catch one massive northern pike or smallmouth bass after another. Another dam near our house, Friberg, had a ten-foot-tall platform with a swinging rope tied to a tree. It was awesome. Imagine climbing up to the top, swinging out over an embankment, and splashing into the water below. I perfected a belly flop with a big splash heard for miles around. In the eight years we lived there, we went to the dam every summer but rarely saw anyone else there. I'd ask people in the nearby town, "Have you ever heard of Friberg?" They'd give me a blank stare.

To be honest, I've seen the same stare at church.

What are we missing? For committed and devoted believers, church can be Powder Ridge or Friberg Dam. Too often, we don't even realize that resurrection power is available to us.

So what is church? It's often no different from the world: broken marriages, extramarital affairs, failed endeavors, dissatisfied parishioners, and lukewarm coffee. What do all these things have in common? In any church that operates under its own power instead of lifeblood, the pastors, elders, lay people, youth group workers, and anyone else who happens to be within its proximity will experience these problems, in one way or another.

A lifeblood church is one that offers a taste of heaven on earth, but we're failed human beings. We don't always live up to that lofty ideal. We're content to make church merely a taste of slightly religious warm feelings. We're afraid to offer the depths and, instead, stick to the shallows.

What if there is a way for the church to operate that is not so crippled and diseased? I'm not talking about the "health and wealth" doctrine that says everyone who attends church should be driving a Mercedes-Benz or something is wrong with their spiritual lives. I'm talking about a church that stands out because the gates of hell will not stand against it, a place where marriages are healed and restored, an institution where services don't always end on time to keep the football fans from giving the pastor a death stare. I'm talking about a church with a different ebb and flow. We can define a lifeblood church as one that makes every decision, runs every program, and serves every person based on the direction of the Holy Spirit—and not for any man-made motivations. It's a church that seeks the leading of the Spirit first, then acts.

The phrase "led by the Holy Spirit" is overused, but it's the only way to define a healthy church. It doesn't have to be a mystical phrase. Being led by the Spirit is mostly about outcome. The goal is to let the Holy Spirit lead—so that God directs the church to become a place of restoration, hope, spiritual fulfillment, victory over sin, accountability to a cause, and sweet unity. Being led means recognizing that real change happens because the Holy Spirit directs.

Yes, a Spirit-led church will face challenging times. The pastor might contract a rare and debilitating disease; the missions team might take a bus that gets stuck on the side of the road in Honduras; the church parking lot might crack and need a fresh layer of asphalt. Life happens.

The conscious decisions we make to mirror the way the world lives, and the materialism and compromise that have become so common among God's people, do not have to exist in a church that embraces lifeblood living. In fact, they won't exist. Pain and suffering are part of the human experience, but the church doesn't need to be broken and ineffective. Materialism in the church comes out of materialism in the heart. Compromise in the church is a sign of compromise in the heart. A healthy church, on the other hand, chooses to let the lifeblood flow.

Think about how God designed the church. In its purest form, a church that functions as the bride of Christ in all its glory—one that is fully and completely operating in the power of the Holy Spirit—will not show the signs of a synthetic institution. It won't be indistinguishable from the local after-school parents' club (except for the wide assortment of powdered-sugar donut holes on Sunday morning).

I've sat in some churches that seemed to think the entire service should run like a school board meeting: dull and lifeless, but at least it starts and ends on time. People need to slap themselves silly after the service so they wake up. We've created a program-driven mentality for how to "do" church, but it's bleeding the life out of everyone who attends. There is a better, healthier way for the church to operate.

In 2002, after my corporate job washed up and I started writing full time, I found out that even the most famous magazines in the world do not always pay on time. I'd write a long feature story for *Popular Mechanics* and go through an excruciating editing process, wait a few weeks or months, and eventually pick up the magazine at Barnes & Noble and see my name in print. Wow! Sadly, many times in those early days I didn't see my name on a check. Since accounting departments took their sweet time paying writers, our bills started to pile up.

I decided to ask our youth pastor if the church needed a part-time youth worker for the middle school program. At the time, my wife and I had four kids of our own, but only one was in middle school—our firstborn daughter, Rachel, who was in seventh grade. I'm sure the senior pastor took pity on me when he agreed to a small monthly stipend. I had no experience as a paid ministry worker, but I dived right in and did my best to lead the group.

Because I had been fired from my corporate job after 9/11 and then spent a few months writing for magazines, my first foray as the middle school youth pastor started right after Christmas in early 2002. It was a rough road. During the day, I wrote articles and hoped someone would get around to paying me. At night and on weekends, I led the youth group of about twenty-five students. I had no idea what I was doing. I'm not gifted when it comes to time management; so during those years, I threw myself into the ministry and also became quite persistent about my writing job. As you can guess, my two jobs pulled me in multiple directions.

I began hearing the parents complain about how disorganized everything was the second half of that school year. I had cobbled together a student worship team but rarely found the time for them to practice. Events that could have had a profound impact on junior high kids felt like they had been organized by the village idiot (that would be me).

My writing career started to gain some momentum, and a few checks came in—enough to pay the bills at least. I committed to spending more time at home, which might have been a blessing to some of the middle school parents who witnessed my thrown-together youth retreats and wondered how anyone survived a weekend away from home with me in charge.

My entire approach to church ministry was to focus on the bare essentials. I remember tracking my time in a spreadsheet, ordering supplies from Sam's Club, arranging for Christian bands to come in and play during youth group, and making sure they had plenty of snack trays. I tweaked the Sunday night program and adjusted the schedule, even though that was obviously not my strong suit. For a typical junior high youth group meeting, should worship come first, then a game, then the message? I had no clue. It was a toss-up on that one. Still, I thought those were important questions to ask.

During meetings with the youth leaders, I focused on things like keeping the students interested enough to come back next week, asking about who was causing disruption and what to do about it, and making sure every leader had a voice about the retreats and other events. My head was in the proverbial sand.

I used my skills from the corporate world to lead by communication, but I was terribly ineffective. I chatted constantly with the youth leaders and figured the parents would give me the benefit of the doubt. I also assumed they would read the postcards I sent in the mail. If anyone had a problem with the group, I figured they'd let me know. We somehow made it through to the last part of the school year, a hopeless train wreck passing itself off as a youth ministry. The parents seemed relieved after the last middle school meeting of the year ended.

And that's when the youth pastor gave me the sad news. Things had worked out okay and he appreciated my persistence (and even more so my availability), but the church would not pay me anymore as a part-time staff member. I needed to clear out my part-time office too. I wasn't going to be leading the junior high group that fall.

It was a devastating blow in some ways. I felt like a failure that had somehow let the church down—the kids, the parents, the church staff, and the full-time youth pastor. That summer, a young intern showed up to take over my job. She had actual training and education from a Bible college. My writing career was ramping up, and I was starting to figure out how to support my family. It seemed like the end of my ministry career.

The summer of 2002 was a pivotal time in my marriage as well. I'll explain more about my struggles in trying to start a music career in the next chapter—and how it ended abruptly when I was recording an album in a studio. At the time, my wife, Rebecca, noted how God wasn't really directing me. My music endeavors were almost entirely based on my own abilities (such as they were).

My wife was on her own spiritual journey, leading Beth Moore studies at our church. For the first time in her life, she started fasting and spent many hours studying the Bible and digging deep into the Word. She was finding her own lifeblood.

During this season, I dealt with some issues related to grumbling and complaining, my anger spiking at times, and overcoming insecurities. In years past, I had built up quite a career as a corporate manager and then watched as it all came crashing down in one afternoon. As a fledgling writer, I'd had trouble seeing how I would ever support my family, even when I'd had the small stipend from our church. At times, we had no idea how to pay our mortgage or even buy groceries for the week. It was easy to see how my half year as a paid youth worker had become mostly about the mechanics of doing the job and getting a paycheck.

That summer of 2002, many of my life goals came to a standstill. This was not a woefully tough time. Friends and family helped us out and bought our groceries on occasion. Yet it was a time of deep introspection. What had made me so interested in doing work at the church in the first place? What had motivated me to even entertain the idea of somehow leading the middle school? Why did I wake up every morning thinking about ministry ideas? That's when I started to tap into something different.

From science, we know that ideas need to percolate in the brain. Neurons start firing, which leads to a random thought, which leads to an actual plan. We might think of this as how coffee grounds need to slowly soak up water. It takes time. In the same way, spiritual thoughts began percolating in my head. I was questioning the nature of my own spiritual reality. A small amount of lifeblood had started to flow, and I yearned to grow deeper in my faith. My wife noticed that I was beginning to burgeon in my spiritual life, finding new purpose and meaning.

At a church picnic that July, I found the youth pastor and spoke to him from the heart. I explained how God was changing my attitude and viewpoint about youth work. I didn't want to see it as a career and didn't want to get paid. My writing was becoming more of a real career for me. I wanted another chance to lead the ministry.

He looked at me a little oddly at first. He knew all about the complaints, the poorly planned retreats, the total lack of ministry success. The middle school group had stayed about the same size under my leadership, around twenty-five kids. There was no reason, in fact, for him to even consider the idea of giving me the position again, paid or unpaid. We stood in an awkward silence for a while. He might not even remember the conversation, but I laid it on the line with him. "I think God wants me to do it," I said.

That was enough for him. He talked to the senior pastor; and by August, I was back to planning some of the events and figuring out who would sing on the worship team.

Everything was different this time. Maybe it was because I had a little more experience, but my focus and motivation had also changed. For the coming school year, I started praying that students would join the youth group and find Christ for the first time. I organized a student leadership team that prayed every Sunday afternoon. It was not a formality. This team, made up of junior high kids, led nearly everything—from our outreach and skit ministries to giving the message and closing out the night with a call for other students to become more involved during the week.

One eighth-grade student must have felt overwhelmed by my trust in him at the time. I delegated many leadership tasks to him, prompted to do so through God's leading in my prayer life. This student gave the message on Sunday nights more than anyone else, including me.

One of the most amazing things about leading the middle school this way is that my daughter Rachel was on that student leadership team. We talked every week about what was working and not working. We made changes not because we wanted a better program but because we wanted to reach more students for Christ. We poured our souls out to God, begging Him to bring in new students each week. The middle school youth program had lifeblood.

After a few weeks of making Christ the focus of the youth group, praying over every decision, and delegating tasks to students, things started to fall into place. I encouraged students to get more involved. I met with leaders over lunch instead of heading to Sam's Club to buy snacks. At one outreach event, the youth pastor gave a message, and at least ten students found Christ and started attending the middle school ministry. Some of those students were in the "popular" group at school and they started bringing their friends. We grew to forty or fifty students. At one of the fall events, we let everyone know that if one hundred students attended a roller-skating party, I would shave my head like a billiard ball up on the stage. One hundred and one students showed up. It is still the one and only time in my life when I had to endure an extremely close head shave.

It's interesting though. I'm not a planner or an administrator, but I still found ways to make everything work. With a newfound outlook about the youth ministry—that it was about lives being changed—I managed to delegate more, find workarounds, include parents more often, and plan better. I worked harder because I had a deeper motivation than before.

By the holiday break, at least sixty students were attending the middle school youth group, and we stayed at that number (or higher) through the end of the year. Many students grew in their faith, others found Christ—it was an incredibly rewarding experience spiritually. I still cherish the memories of when my daughter Rachel and I planned the ministry and talked about what worked and what didn't. She may have rolled her eyes a few times during the student leadership meetings, but we formed a bond during that time that has lasted through her adult years.

One of my favorite verses in the Bible is Acts 4:13: "When they saw the courage of Peter and John and realized that they were unschooled, ordinary men, they were astonished and they took note that these men had been with Jesus." That's lifeblood in action. In my first half year as a youth pastor, I failed to develop a close relationship with Christ. I became distracted by the programs and plans. In my second turn as a youth pastor, I experienced the movement of the Holy Spirit. It started with my own personal time with Jesus each morning, as I pursued a close relationship with Him.

All the amazing things that happened were born out of that deeper relationship. My heart changed, and that heart change birthed a vibrant ministry. There's a model for how this all works in church, of course. You know who gave the best sermons ever? Who ran the best programs? Who had the best administrative staff and the best parishioners? Who shepherded better than anyone? Jesus. He was the best pastor ever, and His disciples went on to build the church.

As we know from early church history, many of the disciples also died on crosses. From what we know through history, Peter died upside down on a cross. Only the apostle John lived long enough to write the last book of the Bible. The disciples had a role model, a leader who always practiced what He preached. It obviously inspired them to do as He did—at great personal sacrifice. After Jesus' resurrection, they had a period of despair; but when the Holy Spirit arrived, they had a new role model.

It's a curious fact of church history that we don't often think of Jesus as a pastor. Of course, there's a difference between a human pastor and Jesus. A pastor points everyone to Jesus, not to him- or herself. Jesus pointed people to Himself. John 17:19 is an amazing verse because it says that Jesus chose to sanctify Himself, which is not exactly something any pastor can do. Maybe another reason we don't always acknowledge the pastoral skills of Jesus is that we like to think of the pastor as a person who gives sermons, runs the elder board meetings, and has the nicest office. Yet Jesus is the true pastor, an example to anyone who leads a church.

Still, Jesus spent hours by Himself, communing with the Father. He sometimes went to quiet places and prayed. No one in the history of the world has had more lifeblood. It spilled out on the cross. That same source of spiritual power is available to us today.

I have a pastor friend who doesn't have an office. How is it possible for him to work? For starters, he works on a laptop. That's one secret. Yet his reasons are much more important than that he has easy access to a wireless connection at church. He doesn't want to miss out on people's lives. By not having an office, he forces himself to walk around, to camp out in public areas of the church.

The pastor at a church my family and I once attended was always anxious and fidgety about being in his office. He yearned to be with people and sometimes sat at a front "welcome area" (on uncomfortable patio furniture) so he could meet people who stopped by the church. He spent many years in Haiti and even adopted three girls from that country. What I remember about him most is that he cared about people, that he longed to be their shepherd. Most shepherds I know avoid mind-numbing meetings about budgets (even if that is a part of the job in both fields), but they are always planning ways to be out with the masses.

Mark Batterson, author and pastor, has said that his favorite ministry location is the church's coffee shop in Washington, DC, called Ebenezer's Coffeehouse. The lifeblood can flow there or in the sanctuary. It can flow when a pastor meets someone at Five Guys Burgers. It can flow when we step onto an airplane and realize a work friend is sitting in aisle 24. "Where two or three are gathered" is the definition of church from Matthew 18:20 (ESV). It even works at Starbucks.

The good news? When a pastor models lifeblood, it catches on with everyone in the church, whether it's in a physical building with a cross out front or at the local gym.

Jesus lived this out for us. He rarely made Himself out to be any different from anyone else. He was fully human. He had hunger pains. He sometimes got tired and needed to sleep. He did not own a home. Yes, He commanded the wind and the waves, but I bet He also got seasick on occasion. His entire goal in ministry was to model what it means to have the lifeblood flowing, to adjust any competing agenda for the kingdom cause.

There's a notable example of this in Mark 5:21–34 about a hemophiliac woman. The story starts this way, as Jesus was on His way to help someone else:

> When Jesus had again crossed over by boat to the other side of the lake, a large crowd gathered around him while he was by the lake. Then one of the synagogue leaders, named Jairus, came, and when he saw Jesus, he fell at his feet. He pleaded earnestly with him, "My little daughter is dying. Please come and put your hands on her so that she will be healed and live." So Jesus went with him. A large crowd followed and pressed around him. (5:21–24)

You'll notice right away that His followers had an agenda. They were on a mission to visit a child who was sick and dying. We can picture the group walking quickly, robes flapping in the wind, the crowd staring at them. "Hurry up, Jesus!" they might have cried.

Then, in verse 25, we find out about a woman who had been bleeding for twelve years. We know more today about this genetic disorder than anyone did at the time of this story, of course. It's a condition in which there is delayed clotting of the blood and prolonged or excessive bleeding. It's typically a lifelong condition. Sadly, the woman had gone to the doctor many times, but her condition only got worse. And she had run out of money, so she was not able to get a new diagnosis. She was desperate.

As Jesus walked by, on His way to help Jairus' daughter, the woman jumped out and touched Jesus' garment. She was healed instantly and the bleeding stopped. In one of the most interesting phrases in the entire Bible, Jesus realized someone had been healed right away because "power had gone out from him" (Mark 5:30) when she touched Him. He asked, "Who touched me?" (5:31). The disciples questioned His ability to perceive things correctly, wondering how He could ask who had touched Him amid so much chaos.

Jesus looked around, scanning the crowd. Finally, the woman confessed to her deed.

While Jesus was looking for the person who had been healed, Jairus' daughter died. Whatever schedule Jesus and His disciples had been on, the incident with the hemophiliac woman had derailed their time. Healing Jairus' daughter had been the primary mission. But couldn't Jesus also stop and heal someone else? Was He restricted by a human agenda that suggests that being late is a cardinal sin?

Perhaps this "optional side quest" to heal the woman meant that people around the disciples started openly wondering if Jesus would be willing to heal anyone else.

Then Jesus gave everyone a lifeblood lesson: "Don't be afraid; just believe" (5:36).

I want to make that my life verse. I want to make that my heart's cry. How about you?

Jesus knew that people's agendas were not as important as living for kingdom purposes. He knew He had to model a kingdom mind-set to earthbound schedule keepers. He drifted off course from their plans, like a shepherd looking for a lost sheep—and that's a good thing. Lifeblood does that to us. It leads us to strange and wonderful things.

To be clear, this doesn't mean that church programs should be run in a haphazard way. Lifeblood is not about making a church more relevant, which just means changing programs to make them more appealing. Lifeblood in church means that programs will run even better, because they are run with an intentionality that comes only when we bathe events in prayer and match up our desires with the outcome that only God can provide through the Holy Spirit.

Let's say the pastor in your church starts following the lifeblood instead of people's agendas. Wonderful! The agenda becomes less important—it is not the end goal. Not that starting a worship service on time is a terrible thing, but hiding behind a laptop all day certainly is. When the pastor moves out from the dark shadow of his or her corner office and starts demonstrating what it means to live under the dominion of the Holy Spirit, churches come alive. Parishioners become more active. Everyone in the community starts to notice. It's a glorious demonstration of supernatural power instead of just a sermon that ends on time and worship songs that are in tune.

Now for the hard part. Lifeblood must catch on with more than a small set of die-hard members; and for that to happen, there has to be an outpouring of the Holy Spirit. The flow must be constant, consistent, and uncorrupted by the world. Some churches operate like I did my first semester as a youth pastor—highly scheduled, regimented, a bit shallow. Other churches operate like I did my second year in ministry—a community of like-minded believers seeking the same goals.

I was fortunate to be engaged in an outpouring like that once. A church community my family was once part of met in a high school cafeteria. A small group of men (and it was always men for some reason) set up the chairs and a portable pulpit every Sunday. Someone with a guitar that was woefully out of tune (i.e., me) would strum a few notes; and long before Chris Tomlin was making music, we'd suffer through a few eighties worship choruses.

This was back when you had to use an overhead projector with transparencies, shining up on a screen. Most of us also boarded a train to get to the school, the women all wore bonnets, and—not really. But it was close.

At first, we didn't have a pastor. The person with the loudest voice and the most commanding presence gave what some might call a sermon, but it was more of a devotional. I'm surprised any of us made it through the service without snickering. Once everything wrapped up, the same group of burly men took down all the chairs and put away the podium.

Yet somehow it worked. And it worked wonderfully.

We all knew each other. Every family was connected by a common purpose to make it through the worship time without laughing aloud when the singers forgot a few of the words. When we finally did hire a pastor, it was only after our community had bonded in a way I've never experienced before or since. When I see people now, years later, who were involved with this church plant, I still see them as close brothers and sisters in Christ, all of us joined in deep communion.

Sometimes friends can reconnect after being apart and pick up a conversation from months or years before. I can meet the people who attended this church now and pick up the same spiritual communion again. It will be exactly like that in heaven—minus the transparencies and stale donuts. It was a church built on a common vision. No one ever put up with the services in the cafeteria for long unless they wanted to be part of the church body, and believe me—they wanted to be part of the church body.

After a few short years, the church outgrew the cafeteria, constructed a building, and hired more staff, but they maintained the same basic unity for many years. When these kinds of bonds form, they tend to stay formed. Like the friendship between David and Jonathan, a lifeblood church stays closely knit. Even when conflicts manifest, when hardships arise, the community cares. We were a community of believers. For the birth of each of my kids, the church was always there—delivering meals, making sure my family was doing okay.

My wife and I raised all four of our kids in that church, until the youngest was in third grade. They were all dedicated up on the stage, like Samuel, and they all became Christians because of how they came into close contact with the lifeblood in that church. They first noticed how my wife and I served there from our devoted hearts. It was the best example I've ever seen of how a church should function—meeting the needs of everyone involved. My kids are all still living for Christ today, mostly because of the Holy Spirit's work in that church.

What was so special about that group? From my vantage point, lifeblood was in our souls. It flowed constantly. Every Christian has lifeblood, but we sometimes stop the flow—whether by our own sin, the distractions of the world, our own skills and talents, or some other means. As Isaiah 59:2 so bluntly says, God is not separated from us; it is our sin that separates us from Him. We are joined with Him; we're inseparable from Him. But sin gets in the way of our relationship with Him. It stunts our growth like a cord around our arms, blocking the steady flow.

I've sometimes had a "check in, check out" mentality at church. I tune in to the mysterious flow of the Spirit during the service or the small-group dinners, then turn it off when I head out to the parking lot. Lifeblood living means that the flow is not a valve we close or a switch we flip.

It wasn't unusual to see someone from the church at the supermarket or a gas station and start talking about the sermon or the plans for an upcoming event. At times an agenda mind-set crept in, and I'm sure people who visited on Sunday did not always feel as welcome as they should have, but we had a distinct sense that this church had been specifically designed to function in a way that modeled Jesus.

One Sunday afternoon, our doorbell at home rang. When I opened the door, the pastor of our church was standing on the doorstep. None of our kids were sick and we didn't have any newborns. We chatted for a few minutes and to this day, I have no idea why he came over. He just wanted to say hello. That's the reason his visit is still so vivid in my memory. *He had no reason for coming over.*

Have you experienced that? The early church becomes the now church. The pastor becomes more than a figurehead; he or she becomes a Christlike example. The church exists to meet the needs of those who attend, and people respond not by some formal agreement or because of a wonderful nursery program but because they sense love. It's a constant flow.

I mentioned Grace Church in Roseville earlier in this chapter. It's a church I happened to visit only because my daughter attended there as a college student. The day I was there, the pastor mentioned how they were expanding their building and redesigning the entryway to minister to more people, because there was currently a lot of confusion about how to find the nursery. It blew me away because I've heard a few "ministry updates" in my day. The pastor explained quite clearly that the church had a heart for the local community. (They even handed out free donuts and coffee at a local bus stop every morning.)

An inner desire drove them to turn their building into a place where it was easier for church attenders to get around and new people to feel more welcome. It didn't come across as a business update. It came across as a lifeblood-driven purpose, a calling to use resources to advance the kingdom. I told my daughter after the service that money must go somewhere in this world. It would either go to help expand the nursery at her church, or to the bank to pay a mortgage or put a nice car in the garage. The pastor had articulated that money was a tool for following the direction of the Spirit.

What I sensed at that church was an excitement and purpose. "Let's build! Let's hand out free donuts! Let's do whatever it takes to reach people for Jesus!"

I want that kind of community again. I've experienced it at times here and there but never quite at the same level as the church plant my family attended. It's a pure taste of heaven, a richly treasured feast. It's seeking God first, then doing a program. It's understanding why we even have a church in the first place and why God wants us to build the church.

PRINCIPLES FOR THE LIFEBLOOD IN OUR CHURCHES

How do you create lifeblood in your church? I've seen four important principles that have contributed to keeping the lifeblood in any ministry or church role.

1. Prayer before, during, and after every activity is vital. Prayer is an afterthought at so many modern churches. And it's often relegated to six o'clock on Sunday mornings for the diehards among us. But it has to be our number one priority.

In his book *Fresh Wind, Fresh Fire*, Brooklyn Tabernacle pastor Jim Cymbala explained how prayer is not just another item to be listed on the weekly schedule. His church was birthed out of prayer, but prayer didn't stop when the church grew into an infant and a teenager. Prayer became a focus and the bulwark for everything in the church, not a prop for the "real" work.

A lack of prayer around any church activity is the clearest sign that no lifeblood is flowing. When prayer becomes a focus, it means everyone involved wants to tap into a source much more powerful and effective than any man-made effort.

2. We should always ask the "why." You know that football extravaganza you're planning with the event team at your church? You might want to wonder about that a little. Is it an outreach event, or do people just like football and tacos? One clear sign that the lifeblood is not in a church is that no one bothers to ask why. We hold the same corn-maze event every fall, we have the toddlers sing an awkward Christmas song at a pageant every December, we can't seem to avoid the "burger surprise" event in the church parking lot every spring. But when we don't ask why when we plan events, we are probably doing them because of some other motivation—getting more people in the door, showing that the church has an amazing sound system, or providing yet another reason to eat food.

Asking why also takes work. It adds an extra step, and many volunteers and staff in church and ministry rarely want to make things more complicated. They wonder, *Why ask why?* "We have always done things this way," they say, or, "This worked once before." The problem with this kind of thinking is that what has worked before may not be the thing that will work again. Asking *why?* forces us to consider whether something is a Holy Spirit–birthed activity. Who was prompted to do this and why? Who are we trying to reach and why? When we ask why, we remove the possibility that we are doing something at church for the wrong reasons.

3. Lifeblood in church makes us less defensive. I love how this principle works. A pastor I knew used to talk about how we should be unoffendable. It was a radical idea because, as a pastor, I'm sure he was offended by people a lot. His comment demonstrated a deep commitment to God in his life. He wanted to operate under the power of the Holy Spirit. When we do that, it's much harder to become defensive or keep a record of offenses, which is a major cause of dysfunction in churches.

I've heard it said that a church split occurs after many years of unaccounted-for offenses and people never apologizing or confessing their offenses to one another. Disunity doesn't happen overnight; it happens when people make small complaints that are never reconciled. Ineffective churches make compromises to keep momentum going but don't do the hard work of resolving offenses.

Let's say you are planning an outreach event in your church with a team of experienced leaders. You have an idea about how to do a group sing-along. Everyone hates the idea. One person on the team tells you that directly. Are you offended? If your main goal is to see the kingdom of God advance, you become open to any ideas that work. You become less interested in making sure your idea works. You become unoffendable. The goal is to reach consensus, because a team that agrees is more effective than a group that is divided.

One way not taking offense is a sign of the lifeblood flowing in the church is this: We won't look for ways to be right about something or get the credit for ourselves. Instead, we will look for ways to let the Holy Spirit move and not get in His way when He does. Maybe our ideas are good ones, maybe we are right; but if we step aside and let other people run with their ideas, the lack of conflict and defensiveness may be the one thing that will help our churches.

4. Success in church is defined as God getting the glory. If we want to know what it means to let the lifeblood in our lives define who we are and what we do, we should look at how we define success in church. When we operate in our own power, it leads to our own success. In church, such an attitude is even more profound because our church success is noticed by everybody. A multitude came to our fall retreat! The elder board praised us for an efficient kids' Sunday school program! We can twist our arms behind us and see if we can pat our own backs on that one, right?

Success in church is hard to define. Does it mean more money in a bank account? More people sitting in the comfortable chairs? Okay, but is that really the goal? The bank is not impressed and no one really notices that we spent big on the nicest chairs. Spiritual success is not even when we see changed lives, as controversial as that sounds. We can attend a prayer meeting for a few weeks and overcome some personal issues and give ourselves the glory. Maybe we're just reacting to the closeness of the group, right? Maybe the community met our needs, but not necessarily because it had anything to do with our faith.

Success is really all about God getting the credit. Think about it. Most of the Old Testament can be summed up this way: The Israelites experienced success on the battlefield, in their personal lives, and with each other because God wanted to show what happens when a nation is tuned in to Abba, Father. The entire book of Exodus, for example, is essentially an advertisement for what happens when we trust in God above earthly rulers. Whenever anyone built an altar in the Old Testament, it was a personal statement about who should get the glory—not a way to cook up some fresh lamb meat. See this fire? The sacrificed lamb? It's all because God did something, and we need to let other nations know how awesome He is.

In church, it works the same way. We should pray and fast, then watch God move. When we forget who should get the glory, we operate under our own power. Success at church happens when we get out of the way and let God work in our ministries to accomplish the unimaginable.

STUDY QUESTIONS

1. What are the signs of a lifeblood church?
2. What does success look like in church? How do you define it?
3. Name a specific example where you've seen lifeblood in your church.
4. What creates a block for lifeblood in church?
5. How can you encourage more lifeblood in your church?
6. Will you commit to praying for your church to have more lifeblood?

4

THE LIFEBLOOD IN OUR MARRIAGES

It was easily one of the most embarrassing moments of my life. I was onstage playing guitar when, in the middle of a song, a string broke. *Thwack!* It was so abrupt and loud that someone in the front row jumped back a little.

It was quite awkward, mostly because I was onstage at a Christian bookstore accompanying a vocalist who was singing one of my own songs. The vocalist looked at me with a scowl because as soon as the string broke, I announced that we would not be able to continue. Most of the song used that string, so it would have been like trying to play a drum set without the snare or a piano using only the black keys. Our gig was over.

We were opening for a Christian artist named Cheri Keaggy, the niece of Phil Keaggy. (Yes, he's the guitar player Ted Nugent presumedly admitted was one of the best in the world.) I don't remember looking out at the crowd or feeling embarrassed by how the set ended. The vocalist didn't like my sudden decision, but there wasn't much I could do. I packed up my guitar and, after a quick debrief with the sound guy and the store manager near the stage, headed to my car. I never stepped on a stage again to play one of my own songs.

That was twenty years ago. So what happened?

I started playing in worship bands in college. Years later, a friend of mine decided to start a band in my church, I decided to start writing my own songs, and eventually my friend's band started performing them. That evolved over time and turned into me playing with a couple of different vocalists. My idea was to perform at churches and coffeehouses and eventually become a professional songwriter with a publishing contract.

During the end of my short-lived career, around the year 2000, I traveled down to Nashville to play in what that town calls a "showcase." I didn't realize it at the time, but a showcase is normally something you do after you've already had quite a few labels or a publisher interested in your music. I had *one* label interested in me, so when it came time for the showcase—which took place at a popular venue with enough space for at least four hundred people—there were only three people in attendance.

One was the sound guy.

One was the label guy.

The third person was my wife, Rebecca, who wasn't happy.

I wanted to write music as a career, but I hadn't quite noticed that only a few people were attending any of the concerts—whether they were with the full band or my duo (me and a vocalist) hammering through a few songs at a coffee shop. We made a CD. About fifteen people purchased it. I knew my music wasn't exactly catching on with the masses; but I had a vision and a goal, and it didn't matter what everyone else thought.

I told myself, *I'm doing the Lord's work.*

Or was I? The truth is, I was doing my own work but trying hard to make things sound spiritual. The songs were about Jesus; the music career was all about me.

Many times my wife reminded me about what it takes to make it in the music business: hard work, perseverance, raw talent. Even if a person has all three of those, he or she may still never end up singing in a stadium in front of thousands. The exceptionally talented among us—those with a rare gift for singing and performing—eventually might find their way to a stage and sell albums. But most of us are not exceptionally talented, even if we do work hard. We're marginally talented, and that's the main problem.

Sometimes I wonder why I kept pursuing music. My mistake was in not listening to my wife, who was taking care of our four kids at home while I was off playing concerts.

The lifeblood flowing in our marriages is like the intimacy we must develop in our personal commitment to Christ, but there can be twice as much flow. If only one person is committed to living the Christian life in a way that does not rely solely on his or her talents and gifts, the marriage can move forward slowly but surely. If both people in a marriage are committed to the idea, it seriously impacts how they see the world, what they pursue as a couple, and what they end up accomplishing in life, at church, and in their occupations. It changes everything.

What was the real problem during my time pursuing music? My wife will tell you plainly and simply: I wasn't thinking about our family. I was thinking about myself. It hurt our marriage relationship at the time, because I focused so much on achieving success in music that I forgot to listen to the one person who could perceive whether my pursuit was really God-ordained.

Pastor Mark Batterson told me once about how mentoring is important because it teaches us about both our weaknesses and our potential. Mentoring is even more important in marriage. Our spouses know us better than anyone else does—our motivations, our dreams, our foibles. A spouse has a unique ability to spot when we are not genuine, when we have a goal that is not realistic, when we are too self-serving. Often it's only our spouses who see our underlying motivations.

In my situation, I wasn't letting the Holy Spirit propel me. I was letting my own dreams and desires propel me. My wife kept reminding me that my pursuits were misguided, but I wasn't about to listen to any of that. I had my agenda and I was going to stick with it.

It's easy as Christians to confuse *our* success with *God's* success. These two kinds of successes are not the same thing. My wife was constantly asking me, "Are you praying about this?" "How is God leading you?" "What answers to prayer have you seen?" At the time, her own journey was taking her deep into prayer and her relationship with Christ; but I was off in left field, singing to mostly empty chairs in small churches somewhere in the middle of Minnesota. Let the irony of that sink in because, other than Prince and Bob Dylan, the state is not known for producing superstars. (There is a paradox in being a songwriter who lacks musical prowess, however, and I'll explain how that worked out for me in a moment.)

The lifeblood in marriage means we do not rely on our own talents and abilities, and we do not rely on a set of marriage rules and best practices. Lifeblood living defines marital success this way: two people living with such deep spiritual purpose that it defines their marriage. Think of the alternative. We might say that a good marriage is defined by intimacy or financial success or effective communication. The problem is, those definitions can exist outside of a deep commitment to Christ. When there is lifeblood in our marriages, it changes how we act toward each other, how we respond to each other, and how we think about the world.

I've heard it said that the Hebrew word for *knowledge* and *action* is one and the same. (Maybe it's uniquely American to separate the two, I'm not sure.) If you know, you act. If you act, then you know. If the lifeblood is enriching our marriages, we will figure out how to listen to our spouses, we will share a common purpose with each other, and we will act differently toward one another. Here's the beauty of this concept: The more we are committed to the call of the Holy Spirit in our lives and living under the power of the blood of Christ, the more power we will have in our marriages. We won't rely on our own strength.

This reminds me of Samson, who was defined by lifeblood. He didn't always trust fully in his Abba, Father, but when he did, look out! That was particularly true if you were a Philistine and you happened to be within a few miles of him and the jawbone he carried around.

My childhood Sunday school teachers forever ruined the story of Samson for me, mostly because they gave the edited safe-for-children version. I'm a child of the seventies. I attended church from an early age, which means I grew up with flannel boards and songs about being happy in Jesus. Along with Noah and the story of Peter walking on the water, Samson was a favorite character of mine—portrayed by my Sunday school teachers as a manly man, a guy who wore a loincloth as if he was in a Fruit of the Loom commercial. First he tore a lion apart. Then he used the jawbone of a donkey to kill a bunch of bad people. Then he met Delilah. (Oops on that one.) The bad people shaved his head and he lost his power, but God restored him at the last minute. The final act always involved a strong guy chained to pillars and pulling them down. No one ever told me anything about Samson being guided by the Holy Spirit, even though a close reading of Judges 13–16 makes it clear that he was. "The Spirit of the LORD began to stir him" is printed right there in Judges 13:25. Who knew? Not me, because that wasn't a phrase we used in Sunday school. We heard a whitewashed version about a burly guy who was tricked by a wily woman. The truth, as usual, is harder to swallow.

Imagine walking into your local "Christian-safe" sports bar at night. Over by the bar, you see a guy with long hair sipping a cold beer. The waiter is trying to avoid him and only occasionally offers him a refill, without looking him in the eyes. The long-haired guy has issues. He barks about this and that. He stands up occasionally and looks at his reflection in the windows. He has an attitude. As you pick and prod at your undercooked chicken filet, you wonder how a guy like that ended up at the sports bar by himself. Suddenly, he saunters over.

"Mind if I squat?" he asks, and then, abruptly, he squats. The guy is staring at you with a thoughtful gaze (or maybe it's a buzz from the beer). With his biceps bulging across the table, he looks a bit like Arnold Schwarzenegger in the first *Conan* movie. He flips his long, brown hair over his shoulder and flashes two dimples on his face.

"Name's Samson," he says with a smirk. "What's your deal?"

You have no idea what to say. Who is this guy? You have a mind-bleach moment and forget about what you learned in Sunday school. You realize Samson is a little full of himself. He keeps flexing and smiling. He keeps looking at his reflection. And that hair? It's annoying.

To me, that's Samson. That's the guy in the Bible.

In Judges 14:2, he speaks for the first time. What's his first utterance? I imagine him having a thick Austrian accent. He tells his parents that he has spotted a Philistine woman in town. "Get her for me," he says. Wait, what? This sounds like a kid who has entitlement issues.

His parents make a counteroffer: "Dude, let us set you straight. We're not going to get anyone for you. You might need a reality check here."

The dumb stare turns into a scowl, and Samson walks off.

The one thing my teachers didn't mention in Sunday school is that Samson was a seriously flawed person, picked by God to defeat an enemy intent on ruling over Israel. Do you see yourself in the story of Samson? I certainly see myself. I've never swung my long, brown hair around my back, but I've certainly had times when my ego became a little hard to manage (maybe you picked that up when I related the story of my music career). Samson might have been able to bench-press two hundred pounds on his own; but the real story is that, with the Holy Spirit guiding him, he accomplished much more. He tore that lion apart like it was a paper bag. Somehow he found three hundred foxes, tied their tails together, attached torches to them, and dispatched them to ruin the Philistine crops. He was a brute force in sandals.

In one of the most curious passages in the entire Bible, we find out that it was, in fact, Samson's long hair that gave him such enormous power. Of course, we know it was really God working through the Holy Spirit. I find it interesting that, at the end of Judges 16, Samson prayed for one last lifeblood moment before he died. Had his hair miraculously grown back? Maybe.

Judges 16:22 does mention his hair again, but really his final act is all about God empowering him.

In many ways, I can find my own story reflected in the story of Samson. I've seen God move in my life so powerfully that the earth seemed to shake. His lifeblood coursing through me, I became a vessel of His incredible power and watched as He moved in the hearts of those around me.

If you really did meet a guy like Samson at a sports bar, you might not know about his true source of power. I believe Samson was vain, but he was also willing to be an instrument of God. He recognized—even with all his obvious faults—that he was not about to rip apart a lion only with his own strength. He may have been handy with a jawbone, but only God could have enabled him to defeat an army by himself. The wonderful thing about this kind of empowerment is that God gets the glory, as He should.

Delilah plays a big part in the story. What was she trying to accomplish? The exact opposite of what we would want to pursue in a marriage defined by lifeblood—Delilah wanted to block Samson's power. She wanted to distract and dissuade him. Some commentators suggest that Delilah was politically motivated, a plant who wanted to make sure Samson didn't cause any more problems for the Philistines. We know one thing for sure. Her schemes worked. It may have taken her a few attempts, but eventually Delilah did stop Samson. She blocked his lifeblood.

Marriages erode in this same way. We lose sight of our real source of power, and we look for alternative pleasures. We open our thinking to new possibilities. We look at our options and decide to pursue something new that is self-ordained, not God-ordained. That's what happened to me. My own (marginal) talent for music distracted me. I wasn't wearing sandals or a loincloth, but I was pursuing something of my own accord.

We sometimes do the same thing in marriage. We make excuses and try to spiritualize our choices, but what we're doing is often all about us: "I'm the breadwinner, therefore I get to make all the decisions." "I'm with the kids all day, so I'm the one who knows what's best for them." Christian marriages are incredibly role driven (the man cleans out the garage, the wife cooks), but our roles can conflict with our abilities and goals (maybe the wife is more organized or the husband is a better cook).

The beauty of letting Christ become the lifeblood in our marriages is that we both draw from only one power source. There's never any confusion about who is empowered to be in charge: We both are. A "perfect" marriage becomes possible because a perfect power enables us. When a marriage falters, it's often because two people start insisting on their individuality.

It turns out that my main motivation for pursuing music was more about seeking my own fame and riches. It sounds shallow now, but I was using the Christian music profession as a springboard to somehow attain notoriety and make more money. It's ridiculous to think about it, but my wife wasn't always aware of these true motivations. She suspected impure motives, but she wanted to be open to my ideas. Something wasn't quite right though. The lifeblood was flowing a little, but there were many signs that I was relying on my own power.

One was that Rebecca and I rarely prayed together as a couple. It was my fault. Over the past ten years, we've corrected this problem, and it has made an incredible difference in our marriage. But back then my pursuits, career, friendships, and even church involvement were distractions for me from our marriage.

Music became "my Delilah." It was a false pursuit. I exchanged a thread that could have been woven into my marriage and could have created an inextricable bond, catapulting me and my wife toward a common spiritual purpose. Instead, I accepted a secular thread. I pursued temporary and short-term gain.

Another sign that I was relying on my own power is that I thought making music was all about my own talent. I rarely talked about the music listener or what he or she might want in a song. This is remarkable because, at the time, I was working as a corporate manager who led a team of customer advocates. We were designing software, and we constantly asked about what the user wanted and needed. But I never brought this concept into my own music. I never thought about tapping into a spiritual power source even as I plugged into an amplifier.

The saddest realization I have now is that living in my own power meant I was not aware of what was happening at home when my wife was taking care of the kids. This is a widespread problem in marriage. One sign that we're relying on our own power is that we tend to be more selfish. We don't pay attention to what anyone else is doing or if anyone else is feeling left out. We're laser-focused on the goal of getting as much attention and recognition as possible. A curious thing happens in a marriage when we rely on our own power: It becomes all about what *we* have achieved, what *we* want in life, how *we* will find fulfillment. Conversely, a curious thing happens with lifeblood—it becomes all about who was behind any success we achieved.

Samson chose a short-term strategy. Delilah's trick worked. Samson became a crippled-up victim of his own compromise. As we read in Judges 16:15–16, Samson finally gave in: "She said to him, 'How can you say, "I love you," when you won't confide in me? This is the third time you have made a fool of me and haven't told me the secret of your great strength.' With such nagging she prodded him day after day until he was sick to death of it."

Samson finally told Delilah about his hair. He gave in and let the lifeblood run dry. He forgot about the power source and tried to find a way to become the life giver instead of the lifeblood receiver. When a marriage is built around two people seeking their own fulfillment, it becomes a perpetual machine: more, more, more. We push hard to reach more fulfillment. Sadly, this type of marriage usually ends with two people never really finding what they were craving. I know how this works. I finally reached the end of my own power.

There's a reason I never performed on stage again: I woke up. I realized how vain a pursuit of music was for me, and I realized that my wife needed me to be home more and play music less. Then God birthed something new in me.

It was around this time that I started working with middle schoolers in a worship band. Maybe you can picture what that would be like—sort of like herding cats at a circus. It was a little chaotic at times. After leading three different worship teams, I can say it was also incredibly fulfilling. God chose the pieces of my life that He wanted to use—my ability to learn songs, my ability to teach guitar chords, and my willingness to be onstage. He retooled and refashioned a desire for music into a tool for ministry, and that is the best thing that can happen.

For some people, having an exceptional skill or talent creates an illusion. The husband is amazingly good at sales, so he takes on extra clients at work and travels more. The wife is a gifted lawyer, so the firm keeps assigning her the toughest cases. I'm not saying we shouldn't use our talents for God's kingdom, but our talents sometimes point to how much we're doing and obscure how much God is doing through us. This is what creates humility: We realize we have talent, but we acknowledge that God is the one who uses our talent for His own glory. We're humbled by the fact that, in comparison to the Creator of the universe, our talents are incomplete.

That's why it's such a problem to try and live the Christian life by a set of rules or by coasting and relying on past spiritual insights. It's not enough. It leads to failure. We get a little confused about whose power we should be relying on as our tanks run dry and we finally reach the end of our abilities.

We all know how this works in a marriage that's one-sided. One spouse is more than willing to give up control to the Holy Spirit and set aside all selfish ambitions, but the other spouse is pursuing the things of the world—like making more money. Thinking back to Delilah, she obviously didn't live according to lifeblood. She never sought wise counsel; and she was not an ally for Samson, ready to encourage him with spiritual conviction.

The Bible makes it clear in Deuteronomy 8:17–18 that this is not the right way to live: "You may say in your heart, 'My power and the strength of my hand made me this wealth.' But you shall remember the LORD your God, for it is He who is giving you power to make wealth, that He may confirm His covenant which He swore to your fathers, as *it is* this day" (NASB).

Our motivations can be a revelation to us. We can't fake lifeblood living. It means both spouses commit to the marriage. If our motivations are off, it means the lifeblood won't flow.

The course of events in my marriage eventually changed for the better. I stopped pursuing music right around the same time my writing career started to become a reality. I was ready. I had learned how to avoid selfish ambition—how to trust my wife and wait for her to offer her support and encouragement. I could trust her, based on what I knew of her through spending time in prayer with her, or reading the Bible together and talking about plans for our own spiritual growth. We were on the same page. We had the same motivation, the same purpose, the same lifeblood. The immense joy of my marriage is that, after the first eight years of faltering, I was able to reset and rekindle our relationship.

One of the sparks for this rekindling was in seeing how God directed my life as a writer.

After 9/11, when my corporate job fizzled, I was out of work. I came home after my boss asked me to step down from my management position. This radical change, which I'll explain later, led to a eventeen-year career as a writer.

When I first lost my job, I asked my wife what we should do. I was baffled, to be honest. Being asked to leave was quite a shock. For about a day, I thought about marching into the office and demanding my job back. I even considered suing the company. It was my wife who sat me down and set me straight.

"Well, you always wanted to be a writer," she said. That was a pivotal moment in our lives.

This time I did things a little differently. We started praying together, which was particularly important because we had no idea how we were going to make ends meet. I didn't care about my own pursuits anymore. I was just hoping to put food on the table and buy gas for the car. By trusting in the lifeblood raging in me and trusting my wife, we came up with a plan. I would pursue writing as a career and put all my time and effort into that goal.

It's funny now. I asked God to honor my work and help me find editors. When a writing job came up that required some small amount of compromise—if the ads in a magazine were a bit too sexual or the topics not morally sound—we prayed about it and decided to move on and look for a different assignment.

Around 2011, I started writing my own online column. I mostly cover business topics like technology, mentoring, and leadership. For the first few months, my column was like a needle in a haystack—people could find it, but they had to look hard. But the lifeblood was at work in me. My wife and I prayed every morning that God would help me find an audience for the column and lead people to find it, one way or another. It was my job to do the challenging work of writing the column, but it was God's job to direct people to it so they could read the column. My wife, Rebecca, always prayed the same phrase: that I would "find favor" with readers.

I won't say that my wife and I have always believed, without any doubt, that writing an online column and praying that God would help me find an audience was the right thing to do. There were times when I went back to my magazine writing assignments. Yet we kept praying and hoping. We kept trusting that if the column was the right career move for me, then God would hear our prayers and see our pure hearts—that He would see my motivations as unselfish. But at a certain point I had to let go. I decided to do my job differently—I decided to stop writing for magazines. I wrote mostly my own thoughts in my daily column and hoped the ideas resonated with people.

Well, they did. I explain it in the next chapter.

This means living out the idea of lifeblood every day in my marriage. Some days I sneak into my office in the morning and skip pouring myself an extra cup of coffee and sitting down at the kitchen table to pray with my wife; but on those days I feel like I'm missing something, like I am using my own power and abilities. The lifeblood in us helps us know that we need to recharge, refocus, redirect.

I can't imagine what would have happened years ago if my marriage had not been defined by lifeblood. Maybe I would have stalled out completely; maybe I'd still be taking on assignments that don't lead to any progress in my career. Maybe I'd still be pursuing music. It's possible I would have become so distracted and disgruntled that I would have taken on one of those assignments for a questionable magazine or website. Who knows?

The danger of living in our own power in marriage is that we're left to our own devices. It means that two people pursue their own interests and ambitions, separate and unequal. Since in this scenario we don't have purpose and meaning, we wander from one objective to the next. We buy cars and houses, we have kids, we go on vacations to Florida, but we haven't tapped into any deeper truths that sustain us through the difficult times in marriage.

So how do you tap into the lifeblood in marriage? Once again, it helps to understand why the blood is so important.

If you ask a doctor about blood, you will hear a lot about the inner workings of the human body. To say that our blood flow is important is an understatement. High blood pressure, for example, is a serious health risk because it means the heart has to work harder to pump blood, and that means—after many years of the heart pumping and pumping—a higher chance of heart disease. The muscle gets a little worn out and needs some help, which is why blood pressure medication exists. The blood flowing through our bodies is critically important. It's why doctors who are wondering about our health do blood tests. They reveal everything they need to know.

Amazingly, even people with serious heart disease can still walk around. They can still drive cars. They can attend church and help in the nursery. But a time bomb is ticking. It may be months or years, but the lack of proper blood circulation will catch up with them.

This is exactly what happens when we don't have lifeblood in marriage. The lack of spiritual blood in our veins makes us ineffective and powerless in our relationships. This deadness means we can still go through the motions and look spiritual to others, but our lifeblood is almost nonexistent. The half dead can lead worship in church. The half dead can get a degree at a Christian college. The half dead can even lead someone to Christ or become pastors of churches.

The one quality they all share—like the person suffering from heart disease—is that they will eventually end up running on fumes. Every movie about zombies eventually ends with the corpses finally dropping dead for good. What does that look like spiritually? I'm talking about spiritual blockage. Without lifeblood, we're walking corpses looking for a hospital bed and an IV.

In any marriage, people are tempted to slip into old habits. Two people shuffle around in the kitchen, grumbling and complaining to each other. Two people sit alone, waiting for their grown children to call. Two people never seek spiritual nourishment, since long ago they abandoned any hope of getting plugged into a local church. They stay married, and that's a good thing, but they take on a dark pallor and smell like dead people. They have lost their lifeblood.

The Bible makes it clear in Zechariah 4:6: "Not by might, nor by power, but by my Spirit, says the LORD of hosts" (ESV).

Read that verse again, would you? Does it apply to marriage? Yes, it does. It's one of the most important verses in Scripture. In my view it's all about who gets the credit. It's okay to have power and might, it's okay to have talents; but the minute we start thinking that it's our power and our ability that enables us to have a good marriage, that's the same minute we get stuck in our relationships.

My wife will tell you I tend to be a driven person. I dive into things with utter conviction and determination, like someone about to train for a triathlon. I don't know what the word "no" means at times and don't like accepting it for an answer. Like ever.

I've had to learn to let go. There are certain things we can't control. My wife and I have four children, so we have seen how this works as they've grown. We can certainly try, but it's only by God's Spirit that some things happen in life. Try all you want to start communicating more; go ahead and apply all those concepts from the marriage seminar. Doing any of those activities without making Christ the focus of our marriages will not work effectively because, in the end, each of us will still have our own goals and agendas.

Here's the beauty of lifeblood in marriage: It takes all the pressure off each spouse, especially when it comes to the whole submission problem. Guess what? We're supposed to submit to Christ first, then to each other. The one who keeps insisting that the other submit is likely not aware of the fact that there is a God of the universe who can snuff both spouses out in an instant. We all need to learn a lot about submission to the One who deserves it.

As a side benefit, this helps with raising kids. Who is really in charge? God. Who should be directing our families? God. It sounds simple, but it's hard because we're always fighting for control. With lifeblood, it's a little strange if we submit to our creator in every area of our lives, seek Him in all decisions, live with an earnest devotion to His will, allow the Holy Spirit to move in our lives in a way that changes us forever—and still try to get into a debate with our spouses about who should be the submissive one in a marriage. It should be a partnership of submission.

You'd think I would have learned enough about that after thirty years of marriage, but I'm still learning, mostly from my mistakes. I'm still yearning to submit to my Savior first. That's the secret. That's the answer.

PRINCIPLES FOR THE LIFEBLOOD IN OUR MARRIAGES

For the lifeblood to flow, we must commit to a few basic truths that will guide any marriage from a purely functional relationship to one that has the Holy Spirit at the center, guiding every decision we make and helping us overcome the pitfalls. Here are a few of them.

1. A marriage built on prayer will last. The statistics don't lie when it comes to marriage. According to the American Psychological Association, 40 to 50 percent of all marriages today end in divorce. That's startling! And as you may already know, this statistic applies to people who call themselves Christians as well. What can change those statistics? Praying with our spouses. Every day.

2. When two agree, there is more power. Maybe you are married and you used the "strand of three cords" analogy during

your ceremony. Good for you! In some marriages, this is purely ceremonial. Two people are "joined together" during the service and then pursue dramatically different careers and goals in life. That intersecting strand with Jesus? Make it intentional. It's a daily routine.

3. We're in this together. I heard this advice in a marriage class once. It's important to tell our spouses how we are feeling. "I feel you are saying that I work too much" is a much better opening line than "Why can't you do more work around the house?" Marriage with lifeblood is all about trust and that shows up in our daily conversations. Our spouses are partners, not competitors. We should be ready to admit failings, hurts, and desires. Make the marriage more about how the other person is feeling and try to understand those feelings.

4. Consistency is key. I've mentioned how my wife and I pray every morning. That's the anchor. We share what we've learned from our personal devotion times as well, and we talk quite a bit about our goals and aspirations. Lifeblood flows when honesty and openness are valued in marriage. The veins are exposed. Out of the depths of our own convictions and desires, and amid our confessions about sin and insecurities, a wellspring bubbles to the surface. We're real with each other.

5. Give it all to Jesus. Problems arise in marriage. That's a given. The question is: Who will resolve our conflicts? As it says in First Corinthians 13:5, love does not keep a record of wrongs. Instead, love hands these wrongs over to Jesus. When my wife and I decided years ago to "let God and let go," we found an entirely new avenue for resolving conflicts and disagreements.

STUDY QUESTIONS

1. Do you have the lifeblood in your marriage? Why or why not?
2. What's one change you could make to let the Holy Spirit guide you in marriage?
3. What's one change your spouse could make?
4. What's one example from your marriage when lifeblood has flowed freely?
5. What can hurt lifeblood in marriage?
6. Will you commit to praying with your spouse daily?

5

THE LIFEBLOOD IN OUR JOBS

The email made me livid. I was boiling over with anger. There may have been steam coming out of my ears. I mean, who was this person to accuse me of being so self-serving and insult my intelligence? I read the email a few times; and each time, I felt increasingly upset. It was like a pang in the back of my neck, slowly growing into a throb. I closed my email program and sat silently for a while.

I was leading a small team of technical writers in the nineties. We had been tasked with taking what other people in the information technology department said and translating it into English for normal people to read. It was a full-time job. Some of the things these developers said! "The data processing algorithm connected to the machine learning analytics engine." What? Say that again, slower this time.

On one project, a techie named Mike explained to me how to use a new application multiple times. I kept asking questions because I didn't understand how the software widget connected to the data processing thingy. By the time we finished our meeting, he looked exhausted and I had a notepad filled with gibberish.

We met again the next day and went through the same steps. I was a Klingon living on the planet Dorkus, and he was the president of "Please Confuse Me with Arcane Language." We didn't get along. I'm not sure if he thought I was a total moron or if he was simply not interested in helping me understand the project, but we failed miserably to communicate on any level.

Being new to the technical writing field, I decided to write up a short user's manual on this application anyway. I worded everything so carefully it could have won an English poetry contest hands down. It didn't seem to matter that the document didn't really make any sense or explain the process correctly. I was writing! My user's manual was completely useless, but at least it was expertly written by a consummate professional.

When I sent it to Mike for approval, I could not have predicted his response. He claimed I was trying to write in a way that would draw attention to myself and that I had no clue about the subject matter. That was a perfectly accurate statement, but I took it personally. I crafted my own email in reply, written with a cadence and tone that would have made Shakespeare proud, and hit "send." I may have accused Mike of acting like a middle schooler. I may have insinuated that he wouldn't know how to explain the process of lighting a campfire if his life depended on it. I insulted him, and I'm not proud of it. Mike did not appreciate this at all.

After several discussions with his boss, then a meeting between our bosses, it was decided that we shouldn't work together ever again. And we never did. Mike left the company a few weeks later. I never apologized for my email back to him. I never made amends.

Oddly, this story is a good example of what can happen in the workplace. We tend to react and defend. We often don't show the fruits of the Spirit but instead squash people into pieces of pulp. The workplace can be an avenue for anger, a place where sarcasm reigns supreme. It doesn't have to be that way. When the lifeblood is at work in us, when we are ready to embrace God's will in our lives, we will act (and react) differently.

Around the late nineties, I was not allowing God to work through me. I was instead trying to dictate everything about my corporate career. Yes, I was a Christian. In my life before then, especially in college and my early years of marriage, I'd had a deep desire to see the lost become found in Christ. But I had somehow become lost myself in the pursuit of success, and eventually it all came crashing down with a heavy thud.

In recent years, I've managed to change course. I've become less reactionary and more thoughtful. I've tempered and toned down my attitude about work—these days my job is nothing more than a means to an end, a way to support my family. I have a higher calling now and it is all about letting God work through me in a way that only He can direct. What follows is my greatest experience of seeing the lifeblood flow. It all started with one article.

My writing career was a little rocky at first, and I found modest success writing for magazines and websites over a ten-year period. I've written for magazines like *Wired*, *Popular Mechanics*, *Christianity Today*, and many others.

My work hasn't been without a few perks. I've visited the Google campus multiple times. I've tested cars and drones and everything in between. Once I was a passenger on a racetrack in a car that drove itself. I've interviewed famous rock stars and astronauts. In total, I've published more than ten thousand articles in major magazines and on websites. It's a little astounding.

Around 2015, something changed.

I wrote an article about how to have a morning routine to help stay productive that I called "This 7-Minute Morning Routine Will Change Your (Work) Life."[1] The article went viral. Around one million people have now read it, and hundreds of people have written to tell me they follow the morning routine in their jobs.

After years of writing, things had started getting a little stale and repetitive. I'd worked as a journalist for ten years straight, rarely stopping to take a breath. Now, with the success of this article, my wife and I started praying for a new direction. What I then started as a sideline opportunity to write a daily column—one that I thought would not amount to much—became an outlet for my business ideas. I'd written for *Inc.* magazine, in print and online, for several years by this time, but my online column went from attracting a niche audience to becoming one that resonates to this day with readers. It started with one article, but every month now several hundred thousand people read the articles that I post once a day or more. It means that this daily column now provides a career for me, one that was completely unexpected. It's the main reason I'm writing this book, because the column has provided a way to free up many hours of the day. I don't have to write for dozens of magazines anymore. I've also stopped testing as many gadgets and gizmos.

The spiritual lesson for me is this: I used to write for magazines that paid a flat rate for each article, but now I'm paid solely by how many people read my articles. It has been an act of faith for three years straight. God heard my prayers and answered.

This has taught me that it's not by my power that I can work as a writer in this way. It is based on whether people find the articles, like and read them, and share them with other readers. If God decides to close that floodgate, so be it. I will praise Him in the good and the bad. I've now "spiritualized" my job in a way that is highly unusual. During those times when I write with too much pride (and too much flowery language), no one pays attention. But when I pray and fast, trusting in the outcome by tapping into the lifeblood and asking God for ideas, publishing my column becomes an exercise in obedience. I pray that God will use what I write daily.

What about you? For many people, such a working arrangement would be incredibly difficult. For an accountant or engineer, it would be hard to accept payment based on whether people like how you did their taxes or if they can safely cross a bridge you designed. Even in a sales role, payment is not based on a person's daily production but on a commission. I'm now paid according to whether my words resonate with readers. There is a way to let the lifeblood flow in a traditional workplace as well.

What if we lived lives in which our one-to-one relationships with Jesus Christ were what birthed our every action and thought at work? What if what we did and said at work was birthed out of our own obedience and calling as described in the Bible? This lifeblood living would then form the basis of how we act and react at work. Instead of setting aside our spiritual lives when we arrive at our favorite parking spots each morning and zip through the front doors of our workplaces, we'd continue living as though we are committed to the lifeblood of Christ all day, even at work.

This takes all the pressure off us. We can rely on the inner lifeblood flowing and trust that God will use us in miraculous ways rather than forcing things.

You may already know Second Corinthians 10:5: "Take every thought captive to obey Christ" (ESV). Doing this seems impossible, and it is—unless we rely on God's power and not our own. This verse offers no magical formula. We trust, pray, and invest. We study Scripture and live each day in obedience to the Father. The result is that we have the power we need for lifeblood.

Obeying Christ in our thoughts is particularly difficult at work, but it starts with a daily commitment to live by the Holy Spirit even when we are in a board meeting or on a sales call. It's a radical thought, to be sure. What if God placed you in that corporate job or in that preschool or in that police car because you have a higher calling to spread the love of Christ to everyone around you?

Think of the alternative—that God didn't place us in our jobs to share our faith. That would mean we were filling in the hours of nine to five with mindless repetition that doesn't matter. The only purpose we would find is when the company springs for some free food in the cafeteria.

It doesn't have to be that way. God does not look the other way when a person punches in at Burger King for the evening shift after taking care of kids all day. He never looks away.

A side comment in a book by Philip Yancey called *Prayer* has stuck with me. Yancey wrote that God is overjoyed when we turn our attention to Him. What does that mean? During our workdays, it means that God is at work—but the way He ministers to people is not something we control or can relate to our exact circumstances. Many of us see our jobs as entirely secular with no spiritual purpose whatsoever. Maybe we tell a coworker about Christ occasionally or invite the boss to a church picnic, yet we often go through our working lives trying to make money to pay the mortgage. That's not something we want on our gravestones, but it is the truth for many of us, including me. I'm guilty of it too.

We sometimes think lifeblood at work means only living a moral life. That's a small part of it. But Christ did not die on a cross and the Holy Spirit did not descend into our hearts and give us spiritual breath so we could decide not to pull a few levers at a slot machine in Las Vegas. There must be more to the Christian life than reading the Bible and then sticking to a moral code at work. Being right about spiritual topics and staying moral—is that all there is to the spiritual life? How utterly depressing, if that's the case. We live and we die, but that's about it.

God has a bigger, better design for us. In our jobs, He wants all of us. He is not content to let us merely type out business reports on a computer keyboard all day. Lifeblood at work is not only about how we react at work. It's not defining the Christian life as not swearing when we stub our toes on the cubicle wall. It's about being a vessel to spread the aroma of Christ over all situations.

Lifeblood at work means looking for every opportunity. Don't see that as pressure—it's meant to be a way of living. We're utterly indwelled. We're overflowing. When an opportunity comes up, we will know what to do. God empowers us at work. Lifeblood is in us and moving; and when coworkers ask about why we seem different, we'll know what to say.

My job has sometimes involved testing cars in remote places. Once I headed out to Los Angeles and drove a bit up the coast in a new car to see how the vehicle performed. On another trip I flew to Phoenix, then up to Portland for another drive through the mountains. (I know. It seems like a tough job).

I usually combined the drives with another business trip to make the most of the expense and time away from my family. One of the most awkward parts of a press drive has been when I've had to find someone to drive with me. Everyone is a stranger, so it reminds me of a middle school dance.

"Ah, hey—do you want to ride with me in the Ford Focus?" I ask.

"No, I'm already riding with Bob. Ask someone else."

This usually happens a few times before I eventually find someone who looks as lost and confused as I do. We team up for the test drive, then compare notes, take photos of the car, and get something to eat before heading back to our hotel rooms.

For my first few trips with a new person, I have kept things professional and courteous. But on one trip, the lifeblood kicked in. It was mostly because I had spent some time reading the Bible alone that morning. I took the opportunity to ask my driving partner some tough questions—not in an aggressive way, but in a way that fit our conversation. I mentioned how I was starting to view cars as big hunks of metal. I explained that there was a lot more to life than being able to test out a new BMW or an Audi.

This happened on other occasions. I'd ask if my riding partners agreed with me about the deeper meaning of life and then find out more about their motivations. I'd get their back stories: Was this job testing cars a lifelong goal of theirs? Or was it a bit stale? What were their life goals? On some of these drives, I'd share my faith and ask about whether the other person had thought about spiritual topics before. On one trip, I was seriously outclassed. My colleague said he had worked for Youth With a Mission most of his life up until then, but had recently switched to writing about cars. He was taking a short break from missions work but planned on getting back into it and investing in the future generation.

A friend of mine named Wayne went on a press drive to test a car once. He struck up a discussion with his driving partner right away and shared what Christ meant in his life. By the time they returned from the route, Wayne had spelled out the entire plan of salvation and had heard the life story (and all the excuses for living a tough life) of his riding partner. It's amazing to think it only took Wayne one business trip to share his faith like that.

Many of us go through the motions at work. Given the opportunity, like I had when testing those cars, we too easily shrink back and make excuses. We're not supposed to share our faith; it's against the rules to ask spiritual questions. While constantly proselytizing in our jobs doesn't make sense, neither does shutting down during every spiritual conversation. When the Holy Spirit tells us to respond to His prompting, it's time to respond—even if we interrupt the break room conversation.

Lifeblood living at work causes monumental shifts. It's amazing to think about! As Christians, we tend to set aside our Holy Spirit promptings at work, even if we still maintain our integrity. But what if that changed? What if we changed? Each day, we might pray that God will lead us to a person who wants to hear about our faith. Each day, God could prepare the hearts of those around us at work to be receptive to our testimonies.

The story of Peter walking on the water in Matthew 14:22–33 is a good example of how we sometimes try to live the Christian life under our own power.

> Immediately Jesus made the disciples get into the boat and go on ahead of him to the other side, while

> he dismissed the crowd. After he had dismissed them, he went up on a mountainside by himself to pray. Later that night, he was there alone, and the boat was already a considerable distance from land, buffeted by the waves because the wind was against it.
>
> Shortly before dawn Jesus went out to them, walking on the lake. When the disciples saw him walking on the lake, they were terrified. "It's a ghost," they said, and cried out in fear.
>
> But Jesus immediately said to them: "Take courage! It is I. Don't be afraid."

As you may know, Peter was the one who acted. The rest of the passage explains:

> "Lord, if it's you," Peter replied, "tell me to come to you on the water."
>
> "Come," he said.
>
> Then Peter got down out of the boat, walked on the water and came toward Jesus. But when he saw the wind, he was afraid and, beginning to sink, cried out, "Lord, save me!"
>
> Immediately Jesus reached out his hand and caught him. "You of little faith," he said, "why did you doubt?"

> And when they climbed into the boat, the wind died down. Then those who were in the boat worshiped him, saying, "Truly you are the Son of God."

What surprises me about these verses is that Peter tried to get out of the boat at all. He saw only Jesus off in the distance, not the raging storm. He didn't step out of the boat in his power—none of us can walk on water. His faith helped him walk toward Jesus. (His lack of faith is what made him sink.)

We don't always live in a way that requires extraordinary faith. We sometimes choose to look at our circumstances, our health, or our relationships instead of Jesus. We evaluate our success based on whether we stay above water or sink. The above passage in Matthew suggests a different way to live in the power of faith: eyes pointed toward the Savior as we keep walking on the water.

I learned a lot about my power versus the power of Christ recently. It all started in Amstetten, a town in the middle of Austria. I had a wonderful plan. After biking all summer at home in Minnesota with my wife, I came up with the idea of biking in Austria with my son-in-law, Jonas, and his dad, Andreas. Why not? We'd have quite the adventure! I would pedal like an Italian cyclist over the Austrian Alps and along the gently flowing rivers as the other two tried to keep up.

That was my plan. Things didn't quite pan out that way.

That previous year, in 2016, I had managed to lose thirty pounds, mostly by eating healthy foods and walking three or four miles per day. As a journalist, I'm always figuring out how to test products and services that will make a difference and help people, and I found one that involved meeting with a weight-loss counselor once per week. My counselor suggested I try biking.

That idea evolved into a bike test and the bike test evolved into multiple camping trips, including one in southern Minnesota. This evolved into testing multiple bikes on multiple trips. By the time I arrived in Austria, I was comfortable biking thirty or forty miles in one day with no problem. Unfortunately, I had never met the Alps of Austria before.

The truth is, Amstetten is not even that close to the Alps, but it's close enough. We started out early one morning, stopped at a McDonald's for coffee, and biked one way about fifteen miles to another town called Waidhofen, which is at least closer to the Alps. (I know it was closer because we eventually started biking up hills that reminded me of San Francisco without the street cars.) It was incredibly challenging and increasingly more difficult.

"Biking back will be easy," I announced enthusiastically.

But I didn't quite realize that the hills would go up and then down again over and over all the way to Waidhofen—and all the way back. We finally returned to Amstetten and decided to keep going to Neuhofen, where my son-in-law's parents live. That was a big mistake.

As we biked the last five miles or so of the route, my energy level dropped like an anchor into the deep, black ocean. I was spent. We found an old farming road that stretched up above Andreas' house, knowing we would have one final downhill ride. As we rode, the sun sank below the horizon, and the forest grew dark and foreboding. This wasn't fun anymore.

"This is the Black Forest of Austria, eh?" I said, trying to lighten my mood.

"You could call it that," said Andreas with a smile. A few years older than me, he barely looked winded. My son-in-law had the jaunty air of someone who could keep riding for a few more kilometers. With each pedal push, I felt as if the air was being pulled out of my lungs.

It was work. How had this happened?

I finally had to dismount and walk beside my bike. The ride was almost over, but my body didn't know that yet. We finally reached the top of the last hill, and we all took a final push off and sailed down to the house. I remember the wind in my hair (what's left of it) and looking to my left at the autobahn off in the distance and the lights from the next town over.

When we finally put our bikes away, I found a chair and flopped down in a heap.

I was completely destroyed. All my abilities, all my talents, and all my labor would not help me get up out of that chair. I was done. The blood coursing through my veins needed to slow down. My heart, beating as if I had competed in a triathlon and not biked thirty miles, was pumping at a furious rate. We drank water and ate crackers, but I could barely move.

"What did we just do?" I asked.

"We biked thirty miles," Jonas said.

"It felt like we biked sixty miles," I insisted. In some ways, we had. The hills had doubled the energy we needed to expend, in comparison to biking on the flat trails of Minnesota. At least that's what I planned to tell everyone. It felt as if we had biked across the entire country.

If you ask a real cyclist about energy depletion, you'll hear about how the body works and that it's important to revitalize during long trips, usually with candy or soda pop. The body constantly manufactures energy and then uses it up. When a person does a workout or runs a marathon, the body reaches a point at which it needs to stop and take a break. The factory can't keep moving.

That was me. A spent factory. It took a good thirty minutes for me to rebound. On the long car ride home, I sucked in air and hoped to find a bed and a pillow quickly.

When I finally regained some energy, I realized how much the bike trip was like the Christian life in the workplace—full of ups and downs. We rise in the morning, we pray and read a verse or two, then we try to figure out how to coast our way through the rest of the work day. My bike trip reminded me of the following passage from Psalm 73:21–26.

> When my heart was grieved
>   and my spirit embittered,
> I was senseless and ignorant;
>   I was a brute beast before you.
>
> Yet I am always with you;
>   you hold me by my right hand.
> You guide me with your counsel,
>   and afterward you will take me into glory.
> Whom have I in heaven but you?
>   And earth has nothing I desire besides you.
> My flesh and my heart may fail,
>   but God is the strength of my heart
>   and my portion forever.

That day on the bike, my flesh and my heart failed me. The only lifter of my soul was the arm of my son-in-law helping me up from the chair after the ride. Yet on that final ride down the hill, a fresh power propelled me, a force strong enough to fill my lungs with oxygen.

That force was gravity, but on that day I called it relief. My power had concluded, and it was time for another power to take over. If it wasn't for gravity pulling me down that final hill to finish the race, I'm not sure I would have made it back.

The power of lifeblood living in our jobs is similar. Various forces are at work, pushing us in different directions. Our personal effort in a job or career only takes us so far—to the top of a mountain, perhaps. For most of us, a career is where the challenge of lifeblood living really hits home.

In his book *Not a Fan*, Kyle Idleman makes this point quite clearly. We are sometimes good Christians at church and around the house, but at work we set aside everything we know about the spiritual thought process and use a different one.

How can I get ahead faster?

Who is standing in my way?

What are the roadblocks stopping me from making more money?

How can I impress people more?

We ask these questions in our hearts, of course—not verbally—so no one can hear us.

At work, it's important for us to analyze our motivations. What do people on the sales team see when they look at us? Maybe it's a cool haircut and designer jeans. Maybe everyone in the accounting department knows we attend church, but our real claim to fame is an ability to hide the numbers behind a complicated spreadsheet in Excel.

Compromise can be easier at work because we might think no one is watching us, yet the lifeblood is vitally important in our workplaces. Left to our own devices, we make Christianity an exercise in perfecting programs and practicing rituals, usually best left to Sundays. But when we're trusting Christ to dwell within us in a way that gives us power to demonstrate real faith, that will play out even at a start-up in San Francisco or a small design firm in Minneapolis. As the song "O the Blood" by Gateway Worship attests (on their album God Be Praised):

> O the blood of Jesus washes me;
> O the blood of Jesus shed for me.
> What a sacrifice that saved my life;
> Yes, the blood, it is my victory.

Think about programmatic Christianity versus lifeblood in a work context. The functions and procedures of Christianity, the five-point programs and theological treatises, often take precedence for us since we can easily set them aside during work hours. That's one of the advantages of fake religion. Since it's not true or personal, it can be highly flexible. In a specific setting—nice chairs, an altar, stained glass windows—we're free to act religious. At work, we can take a break from our faith. We now have a different higher power: the person in the corner office.

After all, no one ever pulled out the wafers and fruit juice during the all-hands marketing powwow. Religion built by human hands follows the rules we humans like to establish and one of the most well-kept rules is that we don't mix religion with work. It's verboten.

The lifeblood? Living and active. Providing the source of true intimacy with Christ. Penetrating deep into our veins. Forming the basis of everything we think and feel. That's a radical faith, one that can't exist apart from the blood of Christ and a spiritual transfusion from Him. Those who speak up at work and share their faith or avoid temptation even when no one is looking or seek to serve those who are less fortunate are propelled by a true source.

The beauty of living this way—being transformed and transfused, even at work—is that we have an inner strength, one birthed at conversion but nurtured daily. The lifeblood means we are less likely to fake our way through the workweek and exist apart from our spiritual calling at church. The light within us shines for all to see, not shielded by our own hands.

God had to work on me when it comes to speaking up about my faith. His work takes place early in the morning when I study and pray. Study of God's Word is not only about what we know intellectually. When reading the Word is a purely intellectual pursuit, our faith falls flat. That means believing the right things about God up until the point when we decide to believe different things. Lifeblood living, on the other hand, is about energy renewal. When we have intimacy with God, we have power. When we have no intimacy with God, we have only knowledge, rituals, and practices that come and go. They turn on and off like Christmas lights.

We might say the right things at the right time in the right setting (with knowledge and insight at our disposal), but the spiritual formation inside us is obstructed. We have all the control. At work, we use this control only when we see fit. This stifles us. There's a flame-throwing torch inside us, but we twist the nozzle off and on. Is there a better way? Yes—letting God control the torch inside us. This is not following a set of practices; rather, it's living by the power of the Holy Spirit. Because we have done the hard work of developing intimacy with God, a light shines.

Think of the process like this. Let's say we want to develop a fruit of the Spirit like patience in our lives. We can read all we want about patience and how people practice it. Still, a seed must grow and produce that fruit. The seed is partly knowledge about patience; but it's mostly the process of nurturing our own quiet obedience, studying the Word, spending time in prayer, and having accountability with other Christians. Patience is like a seed that grows.

The best way to deal with the issue of, say, evangelism at work is to let the seed grow, to nurture it, to commune with our heavenly Father, and then let the fruit grow. People will notice, and we won't have to be constantly preaching and moralizing.

First Peter 3:15 says, "In your hearts revere Christ as Lord. Always be prepared to give an answer to everyone who asks you to give the reason for the hope that you have." We miss the richness of this verse. "In your hearts"—this is the place where lifeblood flows. "Be prepared"—that's not always an action verb. It is definitely not just an accumulation of knowledge. It's mostly a state of being that results from an indwelling of the Holy Spirit in our lives.

Because we are indwelled and sanctified, we are prepared. In many ways it alleviates the responsibility we might feel at work to share our faith and live only a moral life. With lifeblood living, what's inside us springs to life and we don't have to worry about being the one who monitors it. We set aside all responsibility for acting spiritually or fabricating a perfect life for those around us.

Trying to be in control is a sham anyway. We are not perfect; only the Spirit inside us is perfect. Instead, the flame of the Holy Spirit burns brightly. As it says in Jeremiah 20:9, "If I say, 'I will not mention his word / or speak anymore in his name,' / his word is in my heart like a fire, / a fire shut up in my bones. / I am weary of holding it in; / indeed, I cannot."

When Jesus was walking on the road to Emmaus after His resurrection, He met some disciples who failed to notice who He was at first. Yet something burned inside them as Jesus spoke, something that could not be contained or squelched. Luke 24:32 explains it this way: "Were not our hearts burning within us while he talked with us on the road and opened the Scriptures to us?"

When we see ourselves as torches that glow, we realize that God is the one who produces the flame in us. We won't need to torment people, preach to them in the cafeteria line, shove Bible verses down their throats. God's way is a much better way: The torch inside us glows bright when the opportunity arises because God is the one looking for the opportunities, not us.

This happened to me while I was writing this book. I visited a company in Minneapolis to talk about their product. During a meeting, we started discussing our favorite books and one of the people in the meeting mentioned a Christian book. A flame suddenly burst to life inside me, like the pilot light inside a furnace. I mentioned that I was working on a Christian book, which is always followed by a question: "What is it about?" I hadn't intended to talk about my faith in that meeting, but I ended up explaining the concept of lifeblood for twenty minutes.

This is why Second Timothy 4:2 exists. It says, in part, "Be prepared." Did you get that? Our job is to be ready, to watch for the opportunities when the intimacy we've already developed with Christ can become a bright flame. We didn't create the opportunity, but we can respond to it when we see the flame ignite. Part of that equation is having the knowledge we need and the verses memorized. Knowledge becomes a tool to use when the Holy Spirit leads, and nothing more. Those who overstate the importance of knowledge tend to overstate the importance of our own talents. A better way is to see knowledge as preparation for when God wants to use us to advance His glory.

Another part of burning brightly is avoiding sin. Its presence in our lives means we will not be prepared. Sin in our lives means we will have a hard time seeing opportunities that arise. That's what makes sin such a problem for Christians. When we indulge in it, we will not hear from the Holy Spirit. Being consumed with guilt or thoughts of how we will follow through on our sinful plans makes it impossible for us to identify when the Spirit is prompting us to act. In such a condition, our spiritual hypothermia drowns out any possible leading from the Holy Spirit. We are blind and stunted, lost and confused.

That's no way to live. Curiously, it is possible to be blind and stunted but still believe certain doctrines and abide by a certain set of rules. Interestingly, we can sin and still achieve some level of spiritual success. It reminds me of the time my elementary-age son decided to drive a car in a farm field. He could find the accelerator and the brakes, but did he really know anything about driving? He knew the basic rules of the road. Yet he lacked insight and wisdom about the dangers of driving a car. (He also lacked a permit, and yes, I grounded him for a week.)

It's amazing to see how people who are obviously living a sinful life can still present an image of a good Christian. They are okay with driving blind. Yet it's hard to fake spiritual maturity. Sinfulness reveals itself when the sinful person fails to act, does not respond to the Holy Spirit, and sits in a slump of spiritual inactivity, sliding into sin again and again. We know that something isn't quite right. One of the easiest ways to identify when someone is not living for Christ is when we see a failure in that person to respond to God. Like a ghost, this person tends to be lifeless and almost comatose to the promptings of the Spirit.

Hebrews 9:14 explains how to avoid sin quite succinctly: "How much more, then, will the blood of Christ, who through the eternal Spirit offered himself unblemished to God, cleanse our consciences from acts that lead to death, so that we may serve the living God!"

Without the blood, we practice a set of rules and eventually we will fail. The victorious Christian life hinges on this one principle: By our power we don't last long; by God's power sustaining and directing us, we can find victory beyond any measure.

As we see in Hebrews 9, this comes from the sacrifice Christ made for us. Many Christians agree that we're set free (or cleansed) by the blood of Christ, but they don't finish the sentence. We're set free so we can serve and we serve only by the blood that sets us free in the first place. Blood and power are linked together inextricably and eternally. Only with both are we transformed.

In Hebrews 10:16 we find even more hope: "This is the covenant I will make with them / after that time, says the Lord. / I will put my laws in their hearts, / and I will write them on their minds." Put in our hearts! Written on our minds! That's the lifeblood we need in our daily lives, the power to act out our faith at work and not preach about a shallow, rule-oriented religion. What is written in our hearts and minds will spring up and pour out of our mouths. That's what makes the Christian life so exciting. God works within us and we respond.

The alternative is when we try to do the work within us and then, lacking power, sit on our hands and do nothing. This false power leads to inaction and there is nothing quite so false as that.

Hebrews 10:22–24 reminds us why this power leading to action is so important.

> Let us draw near to God with a sincere heart and with the full assurance that faith brings, having our hearts sprinkled to cleanse us from a guilty conscience and having our bodies washed with pure water. Let us hold unswervingly to the hope we profess, for he who promised is faithful. And let us consider how we may spur one another on toward love and good deeds.

The rest of the passage, the famous verse about not forgetting to meet with one another, is the ultimate outcome of the verses that come before it. Draw near. Have a sincere heart. Sprinkled as we are with the cleansing water of the Holy Spirit, we are capable of love and virtuous deeds. Unsprinkled and uncleansed, we are incapable of doing anything but *looking* spiritual.

At times, we will look back to the moment of our salvation or an early morning prayer time. Do the look back! Hebrews 10:32 says, "Remember those earlier days after you had received the light." Why? What's the big deal about the light? Hebrews 10:38 gives the answer: "My righteous one will live by faith." That's the action. A light that merely shines and doesn't guide us to action is a light wasted. Bright lights prompt us to do amazing things. Look for those things. This is what is important for the moment—following the light.

By Hebrews 11, we finally see how the process works. The heading of this chapter in the New International Version says "Faith in Action," and that is the lifeblood, the power of Christ in us. Abel, Enoch, Noah, and Abraham had the lifeblood that led to action. Isaac, Jacob, Joseph, and Moses also obeyed an internal power. They were not led by personal motivation. In Hebrews 11:32–38 we find out where this can lead.

> What more shall I say? I do not have time to tell about Gideon, Barak, Samson and Jephthah, about David and Samuel and the prophets, who through faith conquered kingdoms, administered justice, and gained what was promised; who shut the mouths of lions, quenched the fury of the flames, and escaped the edge of the sword; whose weakness was turned to strength; and who became powerful in battle and routed foreign armies. Women received back their dead, raised to life again. There were others who were tortured, refusing to be released so that they might gain an even better resurrection. Some faced jeers and flogging, and even chains and imprisonment. They were put to death by stoning; they were sawed in two; they were killed by the sword. They went about in sheepskins and goatskins, destitute, persecuted and mistreated—the world was not worthy of them. They wandered in deserts and mountains, living in caves and in holes in the ground.

Did you catch the phrase about turning weakness into strength? The lifeblood tends to make weak people strong. Imagine someone sinking in the water, like Peter walking toward Jesus, who suddenly reaches up and grasps the hand of the Savior. Have you done that? Have you reached out to the Savior, with the power available from the Holy Spirit running strong in your veins? That is the power to change lives. That is the power to restore families.

Some of us shrink back at work. We have to file the business report or complete the marketing project, after all. I'm not saying we should shirk our work responsibilities. But I am saying it is too easy to stifle the power of Christ in our lives at work—to turn away, like Peter denying the Savior when he held up his hand and said, "I don't know this man; he is a stranger to me" (see Matt. 26:69–75). Instead of responding to the power in us, we block it. We deny it.

The workplace is the true test in the end. When the lifeblood is flowing, it empowers us at work in ways we can't even imagine. Conversations will pop up in the lunchroom and during meetings. Our entire demeanor relaxes, not squelched by the pressure to conform or the temptation to indulge our senses. People notice. They ask:

"Why are you smiling?"

"Why do you have so much peace?"

"Why do you seem so different?"

"What power is inside you?"

One story from the Bible drives this point home. It's a little obscure, to say the least. The judges of Israel were like spiritual leaders. They were not quite kings, more like prophets (but not always in the strictest sense). One of them was named Deborah. In Judges 4:5, we find out how she used to sit under a palm tree and judge the people of Israel somewhere in the hill country of Ephraim. One day, she summoned a guy named Barak, who was commanding the army. To me, it seems that he had been more than a little negligent in his job duties.

Deborah asked him, "Has not the Lord, the God of Israel, commanded you, 'Go, gather your men at Mount Tabor, taking 10,000 from the people of Naphtali and the people of Zebulun. And I will draw out Sisera, the general of Jabin's army, to meet you by the river Kishon with his chariots and his troops, and I will give him into your hand'?" (Judg. 4:6–7, esv).

Deborah spoke quite clearly, but Barak did what many of us have done. He hedged his bets. He said he would go only if Deborah went with him. In terms of workplace dynamics, this was a little peculiar. Barak wanted victory at all costs, unless of course the cost involved having to trust in whatever outcome God had planned. The goal was to defeat Sisera, commander of the enemy army, who lived in a town with the unfortunate name of Harosheth-hagoyim. As we see in Judges 4:9, Deborah noted that Barak would see victory over Sisera but that it would not play out the way he envisioned. She laid it all out in exquisite detail and explained to Barak how things would happen if he would only stop trying to control the outcome: "Up! For this is the day in which the Lord has given Sisera into your hand. Does not the Lord go out before you?" (4:14, esv).

Barak was trying to leverage the situation. This story is fraught with inconsistencies as to what he was supposed to do and what he ended up doing. Sisera escaped from the battle and Barak missed his opportunity to subdue him. Instead of Barak finding Sisera and routing the Canaanites, as God (speaking through Deborah) had planned from the beginning, a woman named Jael found Sisera instead—and put a nail through his skull, pinning him to the dirt.

Deborah wanted Barak to lead the army and fight the enemy that day. He was supposed to be the one who killed Sisera, maybe by using a tent spike. His desire to leverage the situation might sound familiar to anyone who has a job.

We want things to go our own way. We want the success, and then we want people to mention that success repeatedly to make sure everyone else knows about it. Because we rely on our own talents, we leverage one thing against the next. In my own career as a writer, I've often leveraged one job against another. If one writing assignment with an editor fails, I can always find another one to pursue. That might be acceptable as a business strategy, but it doesn't work in the spiritual realm.

Proverbs 16:9 talks about how man makes his plans but the Lord directs his steps. Another way of explaining this idea is to recognize that God is the one who provides the leverage. We can pick up a stone, but God can pick up a mountain. Does it make sense then for us to try and leverage that mountain at work for spiritual success? Not really.

Looking for an opportunity to share our faith does not require that we violate a company policy or avoid responsibilities. We need a different view of how to leverage things to obtain our own spiritual success at work. God is the only leverage we need. Our jobs are in His hands. Tomorrow you could walk into work—as I did on a fateful day in late 2001—and discover you do not have a job anymore. What can you leverage then? Who will resolve that one?

Too often we think that our jobs come first and that our spiritual lives must follow suit. Lifeblood living says that we are vessels for the Holy Spirit. In every situation at work, there is a possibility that the Holy Spirit can intervene to leverage things for His purposes. It's true that we are supposed to work hard (see Col. 3:23–24), but that is mostly about our attitudes toward work and is not meant to turn work into an obsession or our highest priority.

A contrarian view would suggest that God is not actively involved in the workplace, that He is only an important guiding force in church or in our home lives. Yet God is active in our lives continually. He never stops being active. He never stops leveraging our circumstances.

Barak didn't understand that. He took matters into his own hands and tried to make sure everything worked out. His faith had limits. As a commander for Israel, he thought success would come partly by his own hand. It rarely happens that way, however.

Lifeblood at work means living without limits. Maybe we won't suddenly become John the Baptist at work, eating locusts and honey in the cafeteria, preaching the good news to the pagans in accounting. Yet with the lifeblood in our veins, we won't have to worry too much about being preachy. God will do the work through us. That guy in accounting will ask about our faith; that friend on the marketing team will express an interest in going to church. We won't have to carry around a big wooden cross or stand on the conference room table and sing Jeremy Camp songs to get people's attention. We'll trust that God will do that part.

Unlike Barak, who hoped there was a way to predict a certain spiritual outcome, we won't bother trying to take control and work things out. God will work through us.

PRINCIPLES FOR THE LIFEBLOOD IN OUR JOBS

The good news? Having a lifeblood outlook about work means we will see God bringing about a transformation in us and we will praise Him for it. Several amazing changes in our attitude will take place at work.

1. No pressure! Like the change that happens in marriage, lifeblood emanates from deep within us like a wellspring, and it's God who does the work. When we practice holy living in the morning over dark roast coffee and bagels, our fellow employees will be able to smell and taste the difference. Instead of acting like we have it all together, we won't bother acting at all. Lifeblood is the rich flow of the Holy Spirit inside us, the daily communion we have with our Savior (as opposed to the Communion we do at church on the first day of every month).

2. No judgment! To be honest, judging others doesn't really work anyway. Maybe the office manager is having an affair with the accountant. Do you really think pointing that out is going to change anything? How about discussing the topic with everyone else at the office? That won't work either. Relying on the Spirit to direct and guide us, based on our own deep commitment to Christ, is enough. It is the aroma of Christ and not the aroma of our judgment.

3. No fear! The bumper sticker has given this phrase a bad name. "No fear" means "full trust." In those lifeblood moments at work, we'll learn to lean on God. We'll know—no doubts or questions—that the leading from the Holy Spirit in our lives is going to lead to great things at work. We'll walk into a meeting believing that we can make a difference. We'll trust that a conversation during a long car ride on the way to a conference will lead to spiritual topics.

STUDY QUESTIONS

1. How do you make sure lifeblood is part of your work life?
2. How do you think lifeblood will provide more opportunities to testify about your faith?
3. How has work proved to be a challenging place for you to witness?
4. What's one change you can make at work to make lifeblood flow?
5. Do you recall a recent story where the Holy Spirit led you at work?
6. Name one person who has benefited from your lifeblood living at work. Why that person?

6

THE LIFEBLOOD IN OUR PARENTING

The sky had darkened into a black shadow. I was walking back from a spot on a frozen lake in Buffalo, Minnesota with my son, Josh. We had dropped a line into the murky depths and he was cold.

"What's wrong, Josh?" I asked on the way home.

He was only six at the time, but he made it clear that he wasn't happy. We hadn't caught any keepers and a stray dog had come a little too close to his fishing hook. (Fortunately the hook fell out on its own.) The darkness of the fishing hole looked like an eternal abyss to Josh's young eyes. The strange calm of a Minnesota winter felt too eerie, too unspoken, too oblique to my son.

I wrote a story about this experience[1] that eventually found its way into a book, but I didn't tell the whole story. I was frustrated that day because I had really wanted to go ice fishing, but I realized that my goals didn't match up too well with my pursuit for the Dad of the Year Award. I had a lofty ideal about what a father should be that didn't quite match the reality of what fatherhood is. It turns out the award doesn't exist, but I often still feel humbled and perplexed by the role.

When we finally arrived home, Josh and I pulled off our boots and sat in the stairwell, drinking hot cocoa together. I told him I was sorry for being so gruff about the day, that we hadn't been able to keep the fishing lines from freezing, that the dog had scared him. I apologized because I knew he didn't really enjoy being out on the ice and maybe we should never have gone.

Josh looked up at me as we sat on the steps and I saw a reflection of myself looking back at me. He would reflect either my frustrations or my apology. He would see someone who either had flaws but owned up to them or someone who tried to hide behind his pride. He would model the behavior of someone who cried out to Jesus in his distress or someone who pretended the distress was nonexistent or not that much of an issue.

I was frustrated the day I wrote the story about Josh and the first time we went ice fishing together. The truth is, over the past twenty-five years of raising kids, I have struggled with many insecurities, overwhelming frustrations, a deep sense of bewilderment, and the fact that there is no written code of conduct or user's manual for parents. Like a man born blind, I reached out my hand to fumble through a dark hallway, believing there was a light somewhere that could guide me and then realizing that my role was not necessarily to lead anyone to the light but to *be the light*. Part of my job is to provide an example and model Christ to my kids at all times.

I didn't always do that. I made plenty of mistakes—too many to count—but my kids eventually came into their own and found Christ. They have all chosen the path of spiritual conviction, which is a tricky thing to do in this dark world.

I know one thing: God does not call us to be perfect parents. He calls us to be lifeblood parents. He calls us to live out what we believe in real time, in front of our kids. When we face challenges in raising kids, it's vitally important to let the lifeblood that is coursing through our spiritual veins become the power we rely on to provide an example of Christ. Believe me, we need it. Rebecca and I have come to see parenting as an act of lifelong spiritual mentoring. It's not easy. The biggest problem with parenting is there are no rules that say you can only have children if you are old and mature. In fact, if you are old and mature, it's less likely—not more likely—that you'll have children. Just ask Abraham and Sarah, the two shining examples in the Bible of what it means to raise kids when we have too many wrinkles.

No parenting test requires us to fill out forms and pass with flying colors: Have you lived in an RV trailer in a Walmart parking lot? You're good to go, sir. Please buy a pack of Pampers next time you stop in the store to warm up from the cold. Did you just graduate from the school of hard knocks with a degree in being stupid? That makes you a perfect candidate to give birth to a helpless infant who needs your constant attention. Welcome to the club.

Parenting often feels like walking an oily tightrope. In front of a large crowd. In your underwear. As grunge rock music blasts in the background. I have slipped off a few times, crashing to the asphalt. My kids have found that to be hilarious. Watching me do anything seemed hilarious to them when they were younger. It was my job to provide comic relief, which I did mostly by standing around and doing nothing as they used the living room wall as a canvas for their crayons. Maybe that was my problem.

I learned a few key lessons. Here's one: If we are going to be examples of Christ to our kids, it's a clever idea to figure out how that works. It goes back to our personal relationships with Christ—the lifeblood that flows when we meet with Him, when we pray, when we do what it says to do in the Bible and don't just pretend to follow Him. The lifeblood in parenting is all about being a mentor who lives out the Christian life for our kids as an act of love. Those of us who are parents don't have the answers to every question, especially the one that asks, "Are we there yet?" on the trip to Grandma's across town. What matters most is how we live, what we say, and what we do with our time. Our priorities become the priorities of our children, whether we like how that works out or not. What we model becomes the norm for our kids.

We hear the "don't sweat the small stuff" advice at parenting seminars. Yet we know that lifeblood is all about those small, quiet moments when we *didn't* slam down our fists on the table and storm out of the room and when we *did* model correct behavior at the church meeting where our teenagers were standing around watching us like hawks.

Here's my favorite story about that. It was a sunny day, and I was on a paddleboat with three of my kids. They were still in grade school. I'm not a small person, so the boat tilted to my side. We had an audacious goal: We wanted to paddle around the entire lake. The problem is, shortly after we set off into the sunset, the rudder on the paddleboat broke. Crisis alert for third graders, right? This was a serious 911 emergency for those who were still wearing shoes with Velcro straps.

"What happens now?" my daughter Hannah asked with a hint of anxiety.

"Well, we should pray," my son, Josh, announced.

So with the sun lowering over the horizon and a few people on the shore wondering why we were adrift, my son prayed like a mighty warrior of God. I can't remember exactly what he said, but it was quite profound for someone who had cried when his goldfish died. After he prayed, I explained to everyone on board that we would drift to shore eventually, which we did. We all felt relieved when I stepped foot onto shore and docked the broken vessel. None of my kids kissed the ground that day in thankfulness, but they probably thought about it.

Did I tell Josh to pray? Not at all. Did he know a verse about praying when things go sideways—quite literally, in our case? Not really. What happened that day was simple: Josh prayed because he had seen my wife and me pray. He knew it was the right thing to do. (For the record, Hannah was about to suggest the same thing. My youngest daughter, Katie, was happy to be back on shore in one piece.) It's not bragging to say that this is what good parenting is all about. It's one thing to tell your kids to pray. It is something else entirely to watch as they pray because they've seen you pray and know that talking to God is the right way to live.

As a dad, I struggled through many years of trying to figure things out; but in the end, the real struggle was to remain consistent in my own prayer life. The real struggle was to memorize a few verses and quote them to my kids. The real struggle was to model Christ.

The hardest part about parenting is not whether we make the perfect decision in every situation but whether we know who to trust to make the perfect decision in every situation. The moment we think parenting is about our abilities and talents—our parenting credentials—is the moment we will fail miserably. It's also the moment we realize that there are no parenting credentials. Instead, it's who we know. That's what separates a good parent from an average parent. If we rely on Christ in our daily lives, we will become examples to our kids. That's because God will be the leader of our homes. God will work through us in miraculous ways.

The original parents had this wrong. Adam and Eve expected there to be more to this life than walking around barefoot in a garden. As John Piper explained in a stirring message at the Passion Conference in 2017, the original sin was really all about wanting more than communion with God. Adam and Eve expected some other miracle of life, some expanded knowledge. Their sin was not being content. It was desiring something more besides the Creator of the universe. I've been tempted myself to look elsewhere for wisdom.

As I've explained, for about eight years I pursued earthly wisdom—shortly after stepping on the first rung of the ladder of success (around 1990) and looking up at the possibilities, long before I became a writer in 2001. This period of my life happened to coincide with the birth of our three youngest kids. (Our oldest child was born before I got a taste for worldly success.) As a young corporate manager, I thought I had to get ahead and make more money to support my young family. My motivations, however, were really more about achieving some form of success, perhaps to impress my father who had become a successful businessman at the time. Maybe I had other motivations like wanting to pay a mortgage or buy a car. My pursuit was still vain. The problem was that I had my own motivations, period. It was, to state the exact opposite of what Rick Warren wrote in the first line of his book *The Purpose Driven Life*, all about me.

In Genesis 3:6–7, we see how this played out for Adam and Eve.

> When the woman saw that the fruit of the tree was good for food and pleasing to the eye, and also desirable for gaining wisdom, she took some and ate it. She also gave some to her husband, who was with her, and he ate it. Then the eyes of both of them were opened, and they realized they were naked; so they sewed fig leaves together and made coverings for themselves.

Inside each of us is a desire for worldly pursuits and a desire for God. This is a human condition, whether a person is a believer or not. We yearn for more. We could call this a glimmer of the eternal, a reflection of heaven. We all possess the image of the Creator, as it says in Genesis 1:27. It is dimmed by sin but still exists in all of us. It's the reason we have a conscience, the reason we can tell good from evil. It's the reason any of us can choose to do good at all in life, even though we are inherently broken and corrupt.

First Corinthians 13:12 says, "Now we see only a reflection as in a mirror; then we shall see face to face. Now I know in part; then I shall know fully, even as I am fully known." As Christians, we are all renewed vessels, "jars of clay" as it says in Second Corinthians 4:7. Inside that vessel is our spirit (the old person) and the Holy Spirit (the new person). The Holy Spirit is living and active inside the believer, but we block the work of the Spirit when we sin. With the lifeblood, living only for Christ and not the world will mean we are not so interested in results. Instead, we will be interested in abiding in Christ and having the Holy Spirit work through us. This must be genuine—we should not decide to abandon all hope in the world and live for Christ merely as an act of parenting. Our kids will see right through such acts anyway. If little Johnny or Sally decides not to walk with Christ when he or she grows up, it won't be because we failed to cover the rules enough or check the box for church attendance enough times. Our responsibility is simply modeling Christ above all, living lives in which the blood of our Savior marks us as devoted followers, and turning from sin as an act of obedience.

We can't guarantee that this modeling will lead to our kids living sanctified and devoted lives. Maybe they will wander. Who knows? Maybe they will join a gang. We might see them on an episode of *America's Most Wanted* (even though that show ended years ago). Our role is to demonstrate what a sold-out life for Jesus means. Our kids decide if that's viable for them. None of this lifeblood living is anything like a formula. Remember, the goal is to let Christ invade our souls, to become so enamored with our Savior that our kids see the flame burning. It's exciting! It's not about correcting every single act of misbehavior.

The lifeblood doesn't stop when we fail to see expected results. We keep living for our one and only—Jesus. We keep praying and stay devoted. We keep our eyes on the ultimate prize of eternity with Jesus. The fruits of the Spirit emanate from an interior life of obedience. Whether our kids see that is up to them (and the Holy Spirit working in their lives). They may also choose to find Jesus and live for Him based on our example. But if they don't, it's not our fault. Of course, this modeling is much more obvious than in other areas of life like work or friendship because our kids are always watching us. They live with us. The "vessel" sometimes drives too fast in traffic, watches prime-time television too often, and complains about the pastor over Sunday brunch. The vessel is always on display. What's inside the vessel is not always so living and active. Sometimes the Spirit's clear direction is hampered by our own ambitions and desires, and it's during those times that the vessel looks a bit cracked. We can polish it up at times, but what's inside always seems to seep out one way or another.

With lifeblood in us, with an abiding relationship with Christ on display—all that instruction we give, all those late-night counseling sessions, all the rules we employ will reflect wise decisions in our parenting. We will be examples to our kids, and we will instruct and discipline them with actions birthed out of close, intimate relationship with God.

Proverbs 22:6 is tucked away in the middle of a passage about humility, fear, and the pursuit of riches. Maybe it makes sense that there's a comment about parenting in it: "Train up a child in the way he should go; / even when he is old he will not depart from it" (ESV). I like to bookend that verse with Deuteronomy 11:19: "Teach [God's words] to your children, talking about them when you sit at home and when you walk along the road, when you lie down and when you get up." That's the prescription for parenting. Be an example.

As youth pastor Mark Gold has explained, this process of imitation and training means that we walk step by step with Christ, and our kids will see how that works in living color. "Put one foot in front of the other," as the old song goes from a seriously outdated Christmas special you've probably never seen. When the lifeblood is guiding us, parenting becomes a testimony about how God is moving and directing us. When the lifeblood is missing or minimal, we're on our own.

The best way to understand what lifeblood in parenting means is to look at biblical examples, because that is where we see the truth about lifeblood emerge. Like me with my son—feeling frustrated about ice fishing, but then apologizing and owning up to my mistakes—we find clear examples of flawed individuals who modeled correct behavior.

One of those role models is a man named Jonah. I love this story because it's also about fishing.

Now from what we know about Jonah, he wasn't a parent—at least, we don't ever hear about his family. But his story reminds me of what it's like to be a mom or a dad. We have a mission, we fail, but the end goal is to do the will of God and act out our faith. We have to stick with our kids along the journey. Like a boat at sea, raising kids has a lot of ups and downs.

The story begins in Jonah 1:1–2: "The word of the LORD came to Jonah son of Amittai: 'Go to the great city of Nineveh and preach against it, because its wickedness has come up before me.'"

Now let's stop right there. That seems like a pretty clear mission. It's about as clear as the path we might expect in parenting when the doctor places a newborn in our lap. We are supposed to train up that child and warn him or her about evil. A perfect parent would probably nod in agreement and get busy saving for the child's college education, brushing up on cooking skills, and taking a course on "How to Learn Patience Quickly" at the local community education center. It's not quite like that though.

My niece recently gave birth, and when my wife and I visited the new parents in the hospital, we saw no professional parenting coaches anywhere in sight. Both the newborn and the new parents had looks of total fascination with the world, which we might easily have confused with bewilderment and gas pains. I never noticed if there was a parenting license lying around. Like Jonah, these two had been sent on a mission right there in the birthing center.

The world is an evil place, but it offers no pedigree program. You'll notice that Jonah made a mistake right away. God directed him to go to one city but Jonah went to another, as though he forgot to tap in the GPS coordinates (been there, done that).

That reminds me of when I was a new father, trying to figure out how to buy diapers. It was a little disconcerting. Diapers are not one size fits all and they come with no instructions. My guess is that Luvs wants us to figure out how they work on our own. I stood in the Walmart aisle for maybe ten minutes trying to figure out baby weights and pricing schemes. Maybe it was the fact that I had not slept all night, but I eventually grabbed the generic brand with a picture of a child that matched my own and hoped for the best.

Anyway, Jonah decided to go to Tarshish on the opposite end of the Mediterranean Sea from Nineveh. For all he knew, it was as far as he could possibly get and still be on the same planet. He probably bought a one-way ticket.

But something special happened when he got on the boat. Jonah realized the error of his ways. Sure, he took a long nap and was below deck where he could safely hide from everyone without being noticed. Eventually, he announced that he served a living God who had given him a mission (sounds a bit like parenting to me, and maybe the crew gave him a deadpan look like my kids often give me). He was not carrying out that mission, however, because a storm was raging outside and would probably kill everyone on board. So he offered up an unusual plan.

He told the crew to throw him overboard so that God would not destroy the boat.

In one of my favorite passages in the entire Bible, we get to listen in on the conversation among the crew. I am sarcastically paraphrasing what they said to each other.

CREWMAN 1: So this Jonah guy is the cause for the storm, but he says it's because God is punishing him. He wants us to throw him overboard. But let me be totally honest with you. If he is really to blame for the storm and his God is causing us this trouble, I'm a little concerned. Just thinking out loud here, but my guess is this God will not be too happy if we kill Jonah.

CREWMAN 2: I can see where you're going with that one.

CREWMAN 1: But we still have this storm problem. I mean, have you seen those clouds? I've seen some bad storms in my time but nothing like this.

CREWMAN 2: So what's your plan?

CREWMAN 1: I say we try to row to shore.

CREWMAN 2: What's your other plan?

CREWMAN 1: I'm serious, let's try it!

Eventually they realize that the whole rowing idea isn't going to pan out and they throw Jonah overboard. We can see how they were weighing the odds. In Jonah 1:10, we find out Jonah had explained to them that he was running from God, so they already knew the backstory.

When I was raising my kids, I sometimes felt like I was playing a dual role. On the one hand, I wanted to be the best father ever and live every moment for the kingdom. At other times, I'd sulk downstairs and watch mindless TV shows when I should have been putting the kids to bed. I was living my own Nineveh-by-way-of-Tarshish journey. I often knew the right path to take but chose a different route. Along the way, as I grabbed a bag of chips and a pop on my way to the living room, I questioned my own thought process.

When my kids were only toddlers, I wrestled with them after work almost every day for an hour or more. We'd have quite the battle royal. I performed a wildly entertaining fake pile driver move on them, and we'd laugh and giggle all evening. Having four kids meant they could split into even teams to tackle the big man, and my wife could referee. We bonded over sweaty faces and gently twisted limbs. It was a blast.

There were nights when I put the kibosh on the festivities because I was too tired, too stressed, too hungry. I did my fair share of guilt parenting, that going-through-the-motions mode when you are too exhausted to speak truth into your elementary-age daughter's life or pull out the checkerboard with your oldest daughter who mostly wants to spend time with Daddy. My biggest regrets as a father have nothing to do with providing wonderful trips to Disney World (too expensive) or buying the finest pieces of clothing at Forever 21 (too impractical). All my regrets are related to those times when I didn't get down on all fours for our version of WrestleMania because my preoccupation with my writing career trumped spending time with my kids.

Did you notice how Jonah was doing his best to follow through on at least a portion of his calling? Maybe he used fumbling words to tell the crew about his missionary plans, but he still told them. He still offered up his life so everyone else on board would live. He still had lifeblood, even in the middle of an ocean, and I firmly believe that this part of the story is incredibly important. He was still on a mission, even if the mission had been sidetracked a few hundred miles out of the way, even if he was in the wrong time zone. Lifeblood is always flowing if we are believers. It never stops when we get sidetracked.

My kids didn't always understand why I was tired—and I'm certainly not making excuses—but the important thing to note is, by the time the next evening came around, I got that wild sense from the Holy Spirit that I really needed to put the laptop away and wrestle with my kids.

We are not graded on whether we reach the destination. We are graded on the journey. If you remember the story my Chinese friend told me about swimming across an ocean, you know we are not supposed to measure our spiritual life according to a set of rules. Did we make it to the other side without sinking? Did we make too many mistakes? Those are not the best questions to ask. The best question is this: Did we let Jesus carry us?

On their way to Tarshish, I like to think the crew decided to open their hearts to the true Creator. The passage says they offered prayers to their own gods; but by the end of the chapter, they were offering prayers and sacrifices to the one true God. Jonah's mission was to go to Nineveh, and even though it was a circuitous route, he was still on a mission. As parents, we will miss the mark. Yet we're still on a mission. We still have a chance to make amends for our mistakes. There are no three-strike rules. Followers of Jesus should keep following, keep modeling, keep pursuing. When I took my six-year-old fishing that day, I had to "keep following" by apologizing to him. That was a strange experience. There I was, an adult saying "I'm sorry" to a first grader. I've lost count of how many times I've apologized to my kids.

One of my greatest joys in life is watching them become adults and noting the times when they decide to apologize to each other or to friends (or to me). I don't pat myself on the back and take credit. I say that they learned it from Jesus. I realize how flawed I am and how often I made mistakes, but I also realize that I was living my life as a flawed human who wanted to let the Holy Spirit have full control.

Of course, the story didn't end when the crew tossed Jonah overboard. In Jonah 2, we find out that a massive fish swallowed him whole. It's no coincidence that Jonah was in the belly of the fish for three days and three nights—we know that's a foreshadowing of how Christ was crucified and buried for three days and three nights. Jesus was entombed in a place just as dank and dark as the belly of a fish.

As for Jonah, we know he was in torment.

> In my distress I called to the LORD,
>   and he answered me.
> From deep in the realm of the dead I called for help,
>   and you listened to my cry.
> You hurled me into the depths,
>   into the very heart of the seas,
>   and the currents swirled about me;
> all your waves and breakers
>   swept over me.
> I said, "I have been banished
>   from your sight;
> yet I will look again
>   toward your holy temple."
> The engulfing waters threatened me,
>   the deep surrounded me;
>   seaweed was wrapped around my head.

To the roots of the mountains I sank down;
the earth beneath barred me in forever.
But you, Lord my God,
brought my life up from the pit.

When my life was ebbing away,
I remembered you, Lord,
and my prayer rose to you,
to your holy temple.

Those who cling to worthless idols
turn away from God's love for them.
But I, with shouts of grateful praise,
will sacrifice to you.
What I have vowed I will make good.
I will say, "Salvation comes from the Lord."
(Jon. 2:1–9)

Did you catch any similarities to parenting? Maybe not; but read it again, especially that last verse. It says, "I have vowed I will make good." In parenting, we need to make the same vow when difficulties arise: I will be a Christlike example to my children. I will apologize for my mistakes. I will make amends. I will change. I will be Christlike.

That's not easy. As a father, I struggle to give the right answer so often that I forget to live the right life. That might seem like semantics, but right actions flow out of a right heart. Good parenting means living a life sold out to our Savior. We'll make mistakes, but they are covered by the blood. Jonah's life "was ebbing away" (note the water reference there), but he remembered his Lord.

My family has moved a few times. One of our moves was from the safety of our hometown to an unfamiliar city across Minnesota. This particular move was the result of a pivotal moment at Camp Shamineau, which has played a big role in our spiritual journey as a family. At a women's retreat there, my wife talked to a pastor's wife who said there was a great need for Christian families to move to her area, where there was a Christian school and several healthy churches.

Because my wife was living in the flow of the Holy Spirit, she heard His voice clearly that day. We needed to move. It wasn't a practical decision by any means. We had four kids in school and family who lived a few miles from us. But by the end of that school year, we had relocated.

For us, it was a Nineveh journey (fortunately, we never ended up in the belly of a fish). It wasn't always easy, and we didn't always follow the blueprint. We faced hardships along the way. We knew we had a calling and we had a destination in mind, but we weren't entirely sure why we needed to make such a big move when our kids were in grade school. My oldest daughter was going to be a junior in high school, so it wasn't the best time to relocate. My youngest daughter was in third grade and had several close friends. My two middle kids were deeply connected with friends and school. Sometimes a Nineveh journey impacts the entire family.

We packed up and moved, and all four of my kids went to that Christian school. Because of one chance encounter, and because my wife was so open to the Spirit's leading in her life (and because she convinced me to consider selling our house and uprooting our lives), we developed new friendships, started a college-age ministry in a town near our new home, and watched as our kids made spiritually sound decisions about life, friendships, and even dating.

The move proved to be the hardest for our youngest daughter. She never quite found close friends again after we relocated. At the same time, if we hadn't moved, my second oldest daughter would have never met her future husband at the mini-golf park where she worked one summer. My son would have never become the chaplain of that Christian school. My wife would have never worked as a dean in the school, impacting countless teenagers in ways that will have eternal effects.

Maybe all that sounds like George Bailey and *It's a Wonderful Life*, but the truth is we never know how the lifeblood will lead us as parents. My family had many highs and lows living in that town; and when we moved across Minnesota again, it was also a difficult decision. My kids grew up seeing us make difficult decisions. Did we show them how to do this in a perfect way? Not really. Sometimes we lived out our own inside-the-dark-belly-of-a-fish metaphors. But our kids would say that their mom and I prayed about decisions, sought wise counsel, and were on a mission to live with purpose and conviction.

During those years of raising our kids, I decided to journal through the entire Bible. I wasn't on the one-year plan. It turned into the ten-year plan. Every morning, I cracked open a crusty ESV study Bible my wife had given me for Christmas and wrote down notes and observations for almost every verse in the passage for that morning. I started in Genesis and worked my way all the way over to Revelation. I made it. I journaled through the entire Bible in ten years and have the proof (several journals) sitting in a dusty drawer somewhere. It was a proud moment when I put the pen down on that last verse in Revelation (the one about not adding anything to Scripture), not because I wanted to pat myself on the back but because I knew I had looked to Jesus for lifeblood nearly every single morning for a decade.

My kids knew it too. Those were the years when my wife and I were raising teenagers. If you have ever had the joy of doing that, you know it requires a lot of help. With lifeblood, we have power. Without lifeblood, parenting turns into relying on our own abilities and decision making.

At times over the past two decades of raising kids, the lifeblood did not flow freely in my life. I was most distracted by work when my kids were younger and I was not writing full time. I was a corporate manager with a sharklike mentality. I didn't just burn bridges with colleagues, I set time bombs on their desks and watched them explode into mushroom clouds. I commuted an hour each way to work, and sometimes I was so tired from climbing the corporate ladder that I had nothing left. I'd slump in a chair. Even back then, the Holy Spirit burned like a flame inside me, resulting from my decision to follow Christ in college. It wasn't burning as brightly, though, until our Nineveh move to that unfamiliar town gave me a kick in my spiritual shins. Starting around 2004 or so, I started to embrace the idea that everything we do is for Christ. I paid attention to whether the lifeblood was flowing, whether the Holy Spirit was active in my life.

When we look back as parents and examine whether we achieved what we set out to do, we might ask: Did we raise godly kids? Did we teach them how to act and talk with conviction and purpose? Did they grow up learning about how the world works and how to behave in public? Those questions are fine, but we should also ask: Did we let the lifeblood flow freely? Did our actions match up with our inner life of conviction and the radical pursuit of a loving Savior? Did the words in our mouths come from souls that were changed forever by the Holy Spirit's power? That's the true measure of fatherhood for me.

It's not about being perfect. It's about loving a perfect Savior. Now for the hard part. We must live this out. Once we decide to let lifeblood flow in our daily lives, in our marriages, in our friendships, at all times—now we have to stick with that plan. We have decided not to be the perfect parent but to model the perfect Savior. We'll make mistakes but will we fess up? Will we own up? Will we *look* up?

PRINCIPLES FOR THE LIFEBLOOD IN OUR PARENTING

If we decide to let the Holy Spirit guide us as parents, we need to keep in mind these basic guidelines.

1. Be genuine. This is not easy. In fact, it's really hard. It's tempting for us to hide our true feelings and mask our hurts. I'm not saying we should share everything with our kids; but it is important to let them see that we are real people, that we have challenges and fears. Our kids can't model a fake persona—if they try, it won't lead to anything worthwhile.

2. Apologize often. Raising our kids, my wife and I had a rule that our kids always had to apologize if they were in the wrong. Maybe it was the only rule we had—that and playing video games for only an hour after supper. Yet the cord that connected us as a family was tight enough to withstand some strain. Apologies reinforce the strand. They add to the connection. They repair hurt and pain.

3. Remember that modeling is a tag team effort. We need to be unified with our spouses in this lifeblood mission—to model

what it means to let the Holy Spirit guide us, to put all our ambitions in life at the foot of the cross. We need to be intentional about that as couples. We need to let our kids see our godly acts of service. In fact, we shouldn't be afraid to plan out exactly how we will model Christ to our kids in genuine ways.

4. Fail in public. Failure is going to happen. We shouldn't keep it a secret. We need to let our kids know when we have failed. Maybe we got angry or didn't deal with a conflict as we should have. It's important for them to see us fail, then apologize and make amends. Living for Christ doesn't mean we will be perfect, but it does mean we will be perfectly willing to admit when we make mistakes.

STUDY QUESTIONS

1. Has parenting been a little stormy for you at times? Why or why not?
2. When your kids think about you as a parent, do they think of Jesus giving you the power you need or do they think you have things pretty well handled on your own?
3. How could you let lifeblood flow more freely as a parent?
4. Have you experienced a parenting crisis in which you relied on Jesus more than your own skills?
5. Are you “inside the whale” right now as a parent? If so, what is God teaching you?
6. Do your kids know that you have lifeblood?

7

THE LIFEBLOOD IN OUR COMMUNITIES

It was early in the morning on January 15, 2009. Captain Chesley "Sully" Sullenberger was piloting an Airbus A320, departing LaGuardia Airport in New York for Charlotte/Douglas International Airport in North Carolina. The plane carried 150 passengers, many of them commuters, plus five crew members.

Shortly after takeoff, birds flew into the windshield of the aircraft and into both engines, causing severe damage. As documented in his book *Highest Duty* and the movie *Sully: Miracle on the Hudson*, Sully had exactly 208 seconds to decide whether to turn the aircraft back to LaGuardia or find an alternate landing strip. As most of us know, he ended up arcing the plane toward the Hudson River. Some would say it was a miracle, since the tilt of the aircraft had to be utterly perfect to land just so on open water, but the book and movie make an interesting point about the odds. Sully stuck the landing because he had flown so many times, carried over a million passengers, and had tacit knowledge about what it took to make an emergency landing.

You might say that nothing could have prepared him for that emergency. Yet he didn't rely only on instinct and guts. He relied on his previous experience operating a passenger jet. Landing on the river was incredibly hard to do, but Sully was a gifted pilot who made the right decision. In hindsight, it almost seems as if he had other options—turning back to the airport or landing somewhere else. For Sully, landing on the Hudson was the only option. I also happen to think the real miracle had nothing to do with Captain Sully. God didn't want the plane to crash.

Our lives follow a similar arc. We experience highs and lows. Yet nothing can prepare us for a bad health report or a sudden accident. When those life events occur—and they will occur—we should rely less on instinct. We must rely on lifeblood.

By now we know that lifeblood is all about devotion, commitment, and communion in our relationship with God. It is a transfusion that takes us from one way of living to another, and it is essential for living the Christian life. We hold communion daily with our Savior. The alternative is a false transfusion—our effort, our will, our power all working toward a goal we set for ourselves. This fake transfusion doesn't work. Sin enters the bloodstream and we are crippled, unable to thrive.

Many of us assume that we can find all the answers in life by sheer effort and persistence. Yet when trials come and our lives spin out of control, the false power that comes from relying on our own efforts will leave us wanting more. We may try to make changes to deal with an emergency situation, but we lack the spiritual transfusion required to make them happen. It's a mystery how the Holy Spirit enables us to live in peace and find spiritual fulfillment and lasting joy; but it's no mystery that true spiritual power comes only from Christ changing us, molding us, and reforming us.

Many of us fall into one of two theological camps. On one side are people who believe that we must do all the work, that God is an enabling force but nothing more. The other camp insists that God does all the work and that we are like pawns on a chessboard. Both camps are wrong. As the apostle Paul explains thoroughly in Colossians 2:6–15 and again in First Corinthians 2, we are in a partnership with God. It's our body and His blood in us.

This struggle to live by God's power plays out in our communities: where we live, where we send our kids to school, at the grocery store up the street. We barely notice those around us when we live under our own power. We're too busy stretching our arms, awkwardly trying to pat ourselves on the back. We focus on our own religious efforts, checking items off a list along the way. Maybe we didn't sin too often today; maybe we helped a neighbor shovel his driveway. We at least moved the peg down the board a little, even if it didn't require too much effort. Yet it's always about what we accomplish.

Ironically, this self-absorption is a sin that inhibits the flow of God's power in our lives. It is also a distraction. Participating in coarse jesting during a round of golf or in gossip at a local hair salon makes us look bad and harms our reputations. We sometimes view it as just a bump in the road as we keep speeding along. There's a reason pride is such an inhibitor: It mixes in with the blood of Jesus and stalls all progress in His name.

Do you believe that sin inhibits you? Do you live like it matters? In those times when I've tried to move a few chess pieces around on my own, the result usually ends up looking like a mess. People believe the illusion in the spiritual life that if we follow a few rules or obey a moral code, we will find fulfillment. In my experience as a recovering controller, it rarely pans out that way. The more control I exhibit and the more success I see in my spiritual life due to keeping a rigid schedule or following the rules, the more I pat my own back.

Our inner life is a bit like an underground spring. In our marriages or close friendships, the wellspring is more noticeable—like a pin prick at the doctor, it doesn't take much to reveal what is happening inside us. A friend can see when we are having a dreadful day; a spouse can tell when we haven't spent time with Jesus. A neighbor? A stranger at the gas station? That requires a little more poking and prodding. To find out whether we're healthy, it might require drawing more blood. We can see a light shining in a room if we are in the room or standing outside, but it's not obvious if we are a block away or even in another town.

What this means for lifeblood is that we must work even harder to reach those in our communities than we do in our close relationships to be examples of Christ and respond when the Holy Spirit directs us.

What's so striking about the "miracle on the Hudson," as the media came to call it, is that a community rescued those passengers stranded on the plane and waiting on the wing (literally). Commercial fishing boats, ferries operated by private companies, and those who were merely out for boating adventures that day all worked together to save everyone on board, including Captain Sully himself. For a city of 8.4 million people, that's quite a surprise. One of my column editors, who has lived her whole life in one small area of New York City, tells me that her community is close-knit and her neighbors are unusually helpful and kind.

There is constant upheaval in America these days: protests, marches, political unrest. We're looking for a savior, but there is only one. We're looking for resolution to tough questions, but it can only come from the Holy Spirit within us. First Corinthians 2 makes this abundantly clear. The chapter explains how there is a "secret and hidden wisdom" (2:7, ESV) in every believer, imparted by the Holy Spirit. The "rulers of this age" do not understand this (2:8) because God has imparted it, not Fox News or the White House pressroom. The Spirit searches the depths of God, a stunning and life-altering revelation, since it enables us to understand the things imparted by God in a way that is not normally possible.

As First Corinthians 2:14 states, "The natural person does not accept the things of the Spirit of God, for they are folly to him, and he is not able to understand them because they are spiritually discerned" (ESV).

We can't fully understand an event like the Hudson water landing. We never will. From a science and engineering perspective, the airplane should have crashed. It was unlikely that it would land on the water. This analogy might be a stretch, but we can think of Sully as a bit like the lifeblood of the Spirit, guiding the journey from LaGuardia to the river in those few seconds. We can wing it and hope things work out or we can rely on the data and information we have, but the Spirit imparts wisdom: "Who has understood the mind of the Lord so as to instruct him? But we have the mind of Christ" (2:16, ESV). That's real power. And when a community comes together, that power is exemplified even further.

I have two stories about community and they are both from Christian camps. The first is an example of a community, breaking down. The other is a story of a community with lifeblood.

I worked as a camp director in northern Minnesota straight out of college. (If you must know, I was a shoe store manager for a while, but the retail world was not a good fit—get it?) As newlyweds of about one year, my wife was six months pregnant with our first child. I was the poster child (or young adult) for the word *newbie*. My wife and I had no clue what we were doing. We took on the role without thinking or praying about it too much—drawn to the beauty of the lakeside views, the opportunity to serve a few hundred kids each week at the camp, and the weekend fishing.

There's nothing quite like the community that forms at Christian camps. They create a bubble of spiritual security, a place where kids can commune with nature and see things a bit more clearly. There's a reason many kids first find Christ at camp. There are no distractions from the camp atmosphere, and the staff designs all the programs and activities (not to mention the music) to form spiritual bonds.

Community moves in cycles. At times in life, we feel a keen sense of community; at other times, the community will feel distant and cold. It's a good analogy for why the lifeblood is so important. The connections we form in a neighborhood, with people at our school or college, and with those who visit the same Walmart we do depend on it. That neighbor who comes over and shovels our driveway in winter is reaching out to us. The strands of connection are either loosely wired or wonderfully intersected. I've lived in four different neighborhoods in my life. Some were amazingly close-knit. Others seemed more like ghost towns. Without community, we tend to feel isolated and alone.

Christian camps are well-suited to emotional connection, but they also create a strong spiritual component. We can form emotional bonds with people in a camp setting; but when a spiritual connection develops, it's beyond friendship and kinship. It's more like a family. That's why my wife and I took the job, hoping to do more than lead programs and order food. We hoped it would become a community. Sadly, the camp community was faltering, and it took us several weeks to realize that we had made a big mistake.

Things started to fall apart almost right away. One of the problems was a camp counselor who seemed to be living a lie. When I first met Tom (not his real name), he appeared to be a gifted counselor: funny, direct, and spiritually mature. He and I drove up to the camp together one sunny day in June 1989, right after I started working there. We talked about my plans for making sure the camp ministry emphasized spiritual growth. I shared about how, as a college student, I had worked at another Christian camp and constantly shared my faith with every camper. I wanted to make sure Tom was on board with the plans.

"I'm more than on board—I already have the same plan!" he announced on our drive.

In a way, it was surprising that we had any counselors sign up for the summer. The pay was extremely low and the camp was in a state of disrepair. Entire cabins looked like no one had painted them since the seventies. Others had structural problems. Camp staff used one large room situated near the kitchen as a place to put all the equipment that wasn't working anymore, along with old carpet rolls someone was keeping for no reason.

When Tom and I arrived at camp that day, we walked around and talked about the work we needed to do to prepare for the kids we expected to arrive in a few weeks. We took stock of which boats were available (and which ones looked like they would still float), the condition of the lawn mowers, and the amount of sports equipment for free time on the field. We discussed the schedule for the week and who would oversee what. Tom had some great ideas, but I could tell even on that first day before the other staff arrived that he was hurting. Something about the way he went from being positive about the camp to talking about his concerns about college that fall and his struggles to stay spiritually pure was concerning to me. It seemed like it was easy for him to connect and then suddenly disconnect.

The rest of the staff arrived; and for the next two weeks, we all bonded and cleaned up the camp as much as possible. We hired a nurse, put the dock in the water, went through safety instructions, and made sure the camp board knew what we were doing. During this time, my spiritual lifeblood started to flow freely. I met with the team and prayed for the kids who would be under our supervision each week. We talked a lot about discipleship and mentoring, how to share Christ with the campers, and ways to encourage growth. My wife and I wanted to let the Holy Spirit lead and the staff seemed on board.

Tom was a key part of those "let the Spirit lead" discussions, one of the many reasons everyone seemed to be unified. He always had a positive point to add and a fresh word of encouragement. We started to form a community not that different from the believers in Acts 2:44–45 who shared their belongings with one another. Our bond wasn't formed because of my amazing talents as a camp director, since I had never done the job before and was fresh out of college. Like no other time in my life, those two weeks of preparing for the campers proved to be incredibly rewarding spiritually because of how all the staff had similar views and goals. I learned many of my toughest lessons about leadership with that team, mostly by making mistakes. They were quick to forgive and I sensed that everyone caught the vision. God was at the center.

Because the camp fees were so reasonable, we tended to attract kids from disadvantaged homes, many of whom had never been to a Christian camp before. The kids liked the fishing and swimming, the evening campfires, and the fact that they were at a beautiful camp in Minnesota. That first week was a little rough, mostly because we had no idea how rough the kids would be. Some of them seemed interested only in making us miserable.

Yet we focused on one thing: building the community. Most of the counselors set aside their egos. It's not like we were proud of the fading paint in the cabins or the fact that some of the steps up to the lodge had cracks in them. But we were missional, unified, and intent on sharing Christ with every camper all week long. We spent many hours praying for the kids. All the staff knew we only had this one chance with the kids each week.

Then something wonderful happened. Every week that summer, a camper either accepted Christ for the first time or made a renewed commitment to Him. It was a bit startling to me. I had seen the Holy Spirit move when I was a counselor, but I had never seen an entire camp become a community like that before (or since). By the end of the summer, according to the records I kept for the campers, at least four hundred kids had become Christians.

Still, while the camp staff was unified, we felt a gnawing sense that the wider community—the camp board, the people who paid the bills—were not as supportive. Something wasn't quite right, and it almost seemed as if we knew that our days were numbered.

One day, the board chairman came to visit. He and I talked briefly about the summer and the astounding spiritual revival we had all experienced. He seemed a little agitated for some reason. He had come to the camp not only to get an update but also to talk to Tom. Shortly after arriving, he excused himself and met with Tom privately. I had no idea what was going on. That was one early warning sign that the community of the camp was not as tight-knit as I thought it was. Later that day, the chairman of the camp talked to me again and told me what was happening. Tom had confided in him that his father was abusive. And beyond that, Tom's dad was the chairman of the organization that owned the camp. I had no idea what that would mean, and I didn't ask too many questions. I focused on the camp and let the chairman handle the issue. That proved to be a big mistake.

At the time, my wife was about seven months pregnant. We had some big plans for the baby and our camp involvement. We met with the camp board in August, after the camp season was over, and talked about some of the repairs we needed to do and equipment we needed to buy. In one of my worst decisions as a leader of anything, I told the board about all the costs involved. Many of them looked at me with a blank stare. Later I found out that the camp was extremely low on funds. It was my job to visit local churches and drum up support, but the camp was already in trouble. I met with a few local pastors, but they had already heard rumors about a fiscal crisis. I hadn't known anything about the financial struggles. The tight-knit community of counselors had led to some amazing spiritual opportunities, but the fractured state of the board destroyed morale for everyone involved (mostly for me).

Then the news came. The chairman of the camp called and said he needed to meet me for lunch that day. I was twenty-three years old and not savvy enough to know that there was only one reason the chairman of a camp would need to meet with the camp director immediately. I told my wife before I left that it would be a free lunch and not to worry.

The lifeblood is essential in marriage, friendship, and many other areas of life. Yet when a community has a Holy Spirit-filled purpose and vision, it's about as sweet as any of us can imagine this side of heaven. It rivals the lifeblood in a church because, while it is made up of a community of believers, it exists outside the four walls of a church building, needs no worship team of any kind, and is active even when no church programs are running. In a community that is purpose-driven for the kingdom, the lifeblood flows. Everyone thrives.

On the other hand, when we cut off lifeblood in a community, it feels like a mass funeral. We connect spiritually but then drift apart. This exacerbates the cold corpse-like pallor that is the sign of a troubled marriage or friendship. Instead of the lifeblood seeping out of two people or a small group of people in a church setting, it runs dry for dozens of people. It's more obvious than in a friendship and more devastating. Everyone in the community suffers. Worse, the community becomes ineffective at reaching those in its neighborhood or city. The light fades, there isn't a signpost to guide anyone, and the trouble becomes obvious to a wide audience. It only gets worse with time.

A story in the Bible (Jonah and the city of Nineveh) helps illustrate what it means when a community collapses. I used this story as an example of being on mission as a parent, but it's a good way to understand community as well. Nineveh was a city of 120,000 people, but it had become corrupt. As I mentioned earlier, all we really know about the evil in the city is that it was enough to "come up before" God (as it says in Jonah 1:2) and that it was so depraved that the entire city earned the label of being evil. Something about the entire community set off spiritual alarms.

Fortunately, as anyone who has read the story knows, Jonah eventually went to the city and spoke to the people about their imminent destruction. The city repented and turned from wickedness, which made Jonah angry. God explained to Jonah that this community of Nineveh, which He had been about to destroy, had rebounded. Lifeblood was now flowing. God had to teach Jonah a lesson about community. Nineveh was a place worth visiting and saving. As a side note, the same could be said about our kids—we should never give up on them, we should be patient, and we should wait for our kids to grow and mature.

This kind of geographically based lifeblood comes up many times in the Bible. Sodom is one of the most appalling examples of lifeblood being completely stunted, a town totally taken over by depravity. If you've ever had the misfortune to visit the seedy area of a major city, you also know that there is a level of spiritual sickness at work. I've visited cities where people have boxes and boxes full of pornographic material on the street corner, and they snap cards showing adult images at others walking by, hoping they'll take one. (When this has happened to me, I have typically said the name of Jesus out loud as a spiritual rebuke.)

It's possible that the spiritual connections formed in a city can create a general spiritual demeanor, a tone that becomes obvious when people visit. For all we know, a city could be a camp of the enemy. Like when Elisha saw the chariots of God in Second Kings 6:17, an army (in this case, an army of angels) could be surrounding a city—causing chaos, disruption, and disunity. Yet we can't see it.

I once experienced what it is like to be around a community of pure evil. I was called in for jury duty; and when I went to the courthouse, I didn't follow the signs closely. I ended up sitting in a room where criminals were waiting for their sentencing. I didn't look around too much, but I felt a growing sense of dread. I finally glanced around enough to notice that everyone looked as if they had spent a night in jail, mostly because they had done exactly that. I quickly found the exit.

The best example of community is in Acts, starting in the second chapter. We find out about a community so connected by lifeblood that they didn't just meet on Sundays. It wasn't a commune in the negative sense (a group of people who cut themselves off from society). It was a community made up of people sharing their possessions and all living in the same area, accountable to pastors and elders, and interested in living for Christ in a way we rarely see in neighborhoods and cities anymore. I've heard of communities in countries like China and Africa where a similar lifeblood moves through each believer and becomes obvious to anyone who lives there.

I've visited a few areas of cities that seemed to exhibit a spiritual fervor. It's happened to me more than once in Las Vegas, which has many churches and Christian radio stations. Maybe a place feels this way because it has a Christian college nearby or has a high percentage of churches or a revival took place there. A person can step on a street corner and sense that the Spirit is alive in that community. Can you explain it? Does it always make sense? Not usually. Yet we can't deny that something is different about the place, that it has a peace so profound it's impossible to ignore. It's almost in the air. A community is like that—a place where people are welcomed with open arms.

That's what made my first camp director experience so difficult for me. The community became broken. No one "shared" anything with one another. There was a total communication breakdown.

I showed up at my meeting with the chairman of the camp in good spirits. My wife and I were in the homestretch of her pregnancy. I could only think about the joy we were about to experience.

The chairman and I decided to meet at a favorite restaurant of mine at the time. The place served home-cooked meals: thick pancakes, coffee that could be used to lubricate a car if needed, real butter from an actual cow. The place was packed but we found a spot in the back.

"I have some bad news for you, John."

The chairman looked as if he had sucked on a lemon. His face was pinched, his teeth clenched. I tried to lighten the mood and made a joke about the rainy weather.

"The board has decided to dismiss you, effective immediately," he said.

I stared back in disbelief. I remember the musty smell of the restaurant, the lively discussions going on in other booths. All I could think about in the moment were my wife and unborn child. I had no job prospects at the time, no opportunity to go back to the family farm (and no family farm to go back to), no chance of picking up a job with a rich uncle down in

Minneapolis. I also had no experience other than working in a shoe store and at the camp. I was clueless and confused—a bad combination.

"This was such an amazing summer, though," I said, my voice breaking.

By the time we both finished our sandwiches, we had come up with a plan. The chairman said we could keep living at the camp until the baby was born, but we didn't need to keep meeting with pastors to ask for donations. We didn't need to do much housekeeping, and we parted with no set plans about whether the camp would continue the next summer.

For me, the community fell completely flat. The camp was obviously in worse shape than I had ever imagined. I knew too much about Tom. The board didn't give me a chance to raise money and find more churches to support it. The financial crisis was real, but my dismissal was suspiciously timed with the recent revelation that Tom had been abused by the director of the ministry—his father. I had become the classic scapegoat, the fall guy.

It was my worst experience of seeing how a broken community operates. No communication, no vision, no direction. In the corporate world, that kind of work dynamic is called *silos*, which means small groups of people don't talk to each other, don't explain themselves, and don't get along.

I drove back to the camp fighting back tears. When I walked into the lodge, my wife could tell something was seriously wrong. One irony of this experience is that my uncle, who owned hotels and restaurants in Nebraska, had just offered to help the camp financially. I had to call him and tell him not to send any more checks. It was hard to accept the news. My wife and I were filled with uncertainty and doubt. That summer, we had both experienced an incredible spiritual revival. Now it seemed as though the spiritual oxygen had left the room.

During this time, God kept speaking to me. I had experienced a community of believers working together. This community—mostly the counselors and staff—had created a lighthouse for anyone in the area, not to mention the four hundred kids who had come to Christ that summer. We ended up staying at the camp longer than a month. Our firstborn daughter, Rachel, arrived in November of that year; and we stayed until Thanksgiving, just a few weeks after her birth. The director of the organization decided to turn off the power to the camp and did not renew a contract with the gas company, so we had to burn wood (and even some books from college) in the fireplace to keep warm. We used candles to see at night.

On Thanksgiving, we moved out of the camp and down to the Twin Cities. We lived with my parents for a few weeks with our newborn. It was a time of spiritual growth for my wife and stress for me as I looked for a job and tried to figure out what to do next. I finally landed a customer service position, which led to a writing job, which led to my writing career.

It took several months, but I eventually learned to value the experience I'd had at that camp. I chose to forgive and forget. I never did find out what happened to Tom.

The experience taught me something about a community that thrives, how valuable it was when all the counselors worked together toward a common purpose. It also taught me what happens when the wider community turns into a catastrophe. Nothing was ever the same for me after that in terms of how I viewed community. I had experienced a vibrant community and then watched as that community imploded. The experience made me question if it was possible to have strong spiritual bonds with a large group of people. Thankfully, a second experience changed my perception.

Communities thrive on a common bond. It's part of what makes us human, this desire to connect with a group outside our family and friends. It's the sinews, the arteries, the veins that hold us together. When it exists, we have people around us who love us and are there to help us. When it doesn't exist, we tend to wallow in despair, unable to find hope. But how do you create this lifeblood? How do you put the pieces together?

One answer is to be intentional about it. For the lifeblood to flow, whether in our personal lives or at church or in community, a critical component is needed. Everyone must be like-minded and focused on the same goal, which is exactly what happened with my staff at camp that summer. It's also what happened when I was a youth pastor for middle schoolers. It does happen. It can be mysterious and unpredictable, but it requires a few necessary ingredients.

For those who are Christians, it's inside our souls. The Holy Spirit is the Helper, the one who guides our lives. We block His guidance when we sin or ignore His promptings. The lifeblood is still there, flowing in a way that cannot be denied. As it says in Deuteronomy 30:14, "The word is very near you; it is in your mouth and in your heart so you may obey it." Do we listen to the voice of the Holy Spirit? Not always. We make our own plans at times. We choose our own direction. The lifeblood inside us can heal and restore us.

Often we seek peace from external sources. If we just get that big promotion, we'll be happy. If we can make it past the next doctor visit and get a clean bill of health. If we can last until next month when we take a vacation. But this is peace from without. Jesus said in John 14:27 that He is the peace giver. This peace is "not as the world gives" (ESV).

The world tries to give us peace. That's why Las Vegas, Red Lobster, and Disney World exist. But you can't salve the soul with poker chips, crab cakes, or jungle rides. It doesn't work. This peace from without is no match for peace from within, where the Creator of the universe can invade like no other force and change our identity into one like Christ. Identity change is a supernatural act, one that we're not capable of doing on our own.

Only Christ can supernaturally invade our bloodstream and renew us; only Christ can change fear into love. We can try, but it will always lead to misery and failure. With Christ, we can have victory. We can have peace.

Chris Tomlin writes about this in the song "Jesus."

> There is a truth older than the ages;
> There is a promise of things yet to come;
> There is one, born for our salvation:
> Jesus.
>
> There is a light that overwhelms the darkness;
> There is a kingdom that forever reigns;
> There is freedom from the chains that bind us:
> Jesus, Jesus.
>
> Who walks on the waters,
> Who speaks to the sea,
> Who stands in the fire beside me.

He roars like a lion;
He bled as the Lamb;
He carries my healing in His hands:
Jesus.

There is a name I call in times of trouble;
There is a song that comforts in the night;
There is a voice that calms the storm that rages:
He is Jesus, Jesus.

Messiah, my Savior,
There is power in Your name;
You're my rock and my redeemer;
There is power in Your name,
In Your name.

That's real power. That's lasting peace. He carries us. He heals us. He restores us. He cleanses us.

Real Christlike living is impossible without the lifeblood to change us. We will never find peace at the backyard barbecue apart from the Holy Spirit working in our lives. That peaceful feeling might just be the Omaha steaks in your stomach. But a peace that comes from a newly created spiritual man and woman is attainable. The old is thrown away, left at the altar. The new is here, spiritually formed and meant to serve God and others. It's all spelled out in Acts 2:42–47.

The early church made its community a vibrant spiritual center. Everyone noticed. The believers broke bread together and dove into the Word. They dwelled in abundant community with each other, bonded by an insatiable desire to go deeper. That was a community meant to draw people in, and it worked. The lifeblood in community means there is an inner power indwelling those who are part of the group that emanates outward to anyone in the vicinity.

In this kind of community, peace is like a lighthouse off in the distance. We hear about it in whispers. We look up and it's there. If we reach out our hands, we can touch it. There is no mistaking this community as anything but Christ-centered and Christ-focused. No serving merely to get extra credit points with the pastor, and no good deeds that begin and end with our own abilities. There is only the light of heaven at the center, shining through the soul of every person.

This is the community described in Acts, and it can be the community where we live. But how do we turn a passion for our neighbors into something that shines? How do we join with others who have an inner light or personal lifeblood into community lifeblood? The answer is in James 1.

In this passage, we find a recipe for lifeblood living in a community. It speaks of a community, in this case the early church. Notice how many times James uses the word *we*. James 1:18 reads, "He brought us forth by the word of truth, that we should be a kind of firstfruits" (ESV). Then James 1:21 says we are to "receive . . . the implanted word" (ESV).

Communities change by the implanted word. It is a seed that grows. James 1:5 tells us to ask for wisdom. Without wisdom, we won't act much like Christians. We'll try to do things for our communities and our neighbors, but we'll lack power.

The world does not ask God for wisdom, by the way. The world tells us to act first and worry about it later, to gain wisdom by making mistakes. That's not lifeblood. We must do the hard work of attaining wisdom as a community and then act based on that profound understanding. We are to meditate on the truths of Scripture, to break bread together, to pray. Then, according to Acts 2, we are to go out into the world fully prepared for all the challenges we will face.

John 14:26 says, "The Helper . . . will teach you all things" (ESV). What's the opposite of that? Trying to do everything ourselves and then seeking answers after we screw up. That same verse says that the Holy Spirit will "bring to [our] remembrance" (ESV) the things we already know. How do we remember something we haven't bothered to study and learn? Apart from the wonderful connection to Communion and the blood of Christ that comes with the word *remembrance*, this word is a constant reminder in our daily lives to embrace truth and choose to dwell with our Savior.

What we know, we will do. What we call to mind will be the thing that helps us.

Christian artist JJ Heller has written in her blog that the way to overcome the trials of the world and the anxiety and stress that come into our lives is to speak truth to ourselves—to *remember.*[1] To be so indwelled with the things of God that the things out of our control don't faze us. We must remind ourselves of simple truths like this one from Nehemiah 8:10: "The joy of the LORD is your strength." Do you need that strength? Then remember the joy of the Lord.

When we choose to have joy, we will find the strength we need to share Christ with a neighbor or avoid the temptation of living in isolation, locking the doors and hiding in our houses while everyone around us lives apart from a Savior. First John 4:18 says, "Perfect love drives out fear."

We choose the power of the cross to sustain us. No magical formulas, no ten-point plans, no how-to guides. Rather, we embrace the perfect indwelling nature of the Spirit inside our imperfect natures, driving us to victory. The early church built a community based on prayer, breaking bread, and communion with one another. We forsake that concept to our own detriment, a loss to everyone around us. Fortunately, there is hope. Community can thrive when the lifeblood flows.

Herb Bloomquist was in good spirits the morning of March 8, 2015. As the executive director of Shamineau Ministries, which runs a Christian camp and outfitter ministry with two locations in Minnesota, he was used to feeling tired on the tail end of a retreat. This Sunday, he thought, would be no different from any other. After a hot brunch with a group of hungry guys, the men would all pile into a bus and head home, spiritually refreshed.

He reached for a platter of eggs and slumped toward the buffet table. He was having a heart attack. Two men standing nearby caught him before he face-planted on the table. The camp, located in the middle of Minnesota on a lake, was far from any major hospital, so a few staff members fully trained as EMTs started doing CPR right away. The other men, shocked by what they were witnessing, circled up into prayer groups.

Herb's brother had died from a heart attack just six months earlier; and his close friend, a retired fireman, was one of the first to respond when Herb was having one as well. Another man, a board member for the camp who was also on hand, called for the ambulance. Program director Jeff Cueva and facilities director Kyle Strickland administered CPR and rescue breathing. Herb was out cold and he stayed that way for two days straight.

He was airlifted to a hospital, and when he finally regained consciousness—after multiple surgeries repairing most of his broken ribs—he looked up to see his former pastor and three camp interns smiling at him. I asked Herb to explain what this was like. "You need to understand that these guys are spiritual giants; and physically, they're mountains," he told me. "They would be an intimidating group in any crowd, and I remember waking up and seeing them and thinking, *I am safe*. Knowing the spiritual authority of these guys, I thought, "*There's not a demon for miles and miles around this hospital that would dare approach this place.*""

Herb recovered slowly. Eventually, his wife started a CaringBridge site for people to express their thoughts. At last count, it had recorded 25,610 visits and hundreds of comments. One local business owner found out that Herb and his wife, Debbie, liked M&Ms and gave them a six-month supply.

When Herb returned to work (after a six-month recovery), his staff rallied around him, asking him constantly if he needed help and offering to fill in for him around the camp. "I'm humbled to say that they love me and that this impacted them. For a while, they thought a family member (me) was being taken from them. I have inadvertently scared them several times since," he recalled from the incident. "If I'm down on my hands and knees weeding a garden or scrubbing a toilet and they happen upon me, they panic and come running thinking I've collapsed from another heart attack. It's funny now; but the first few times I really did see panic in their eyes, and it moves me that they love me. I do not think I deserve it."

Herb now thinks he has a form of spiritual amnesia regarding the incident. All he knows is that the community at the camp—the EMTs on staff, the men at the retreat, the interns and local pastors, even people like me who knew him only as the boss for my own kids who have served as counselors there—were praying for him and supporting him through the entire ordeal.

To me, that's a community with lifeblood flowing through it. It's one reason I wrote part of this book at Camp Shamineau in the dead of winter on an island by myself. It's one reason I still visit the camp on occasion with the middle school youth group at my church. All my kids have served at the camp and have made lifelong friends there. (My oldest daughter met her husband there.) When a Christian community thrives, there is nothing quite like it.

You can imagine the support Herb received, when those men caught him near the buffet line and then when others spoke prayers on his behalf. Most of us don't like to be carried. We want to be self-sufficient. Yet our pride only takes us so far. Lifeblood in community means we don't rely on our own faculties. We rely on a group of believers, similar to what we experience at church but with a wider net. Many of the Camp Shamineau staff are trained as EMTs, not because they like the high-tech walkie-talkies and free helicopter rides that go with the role but because they want to be tied closely to the local community around them. It's an intentional act.

Communities form when multiple people have the same vision and goals, and this is always God ordained—even when unbelievers are involved. As humans, we are a glimmer of the eternal. We are designed for connection with one another. When Christians become part of a community, we demonstrate what God wants to accomplish through us on this planet and what He has already accomplished through the Trinity, a spiritual union unlike any other. We might call it a spiritual geography.

This is one reason the idea of a hometown exists, a place where we belong and feel closely connected to others. Lifeblood is, in the same way, the spiritual link that forms between believers.

The unity that comes from friendship and marriage and with our own children and with the church can blossom and become a wider, more far-reaching entity called community.

PRINCIPLES FOR THE LIFEBLOOD IN OUR COMMUNITIES

In the end, a community is a geographic place where we are surrounded by witnesses who provide trust, peace, support, and guidance. Like Herb experienced with his camp staff, it creates a sense that we are being held up by people who love us. How do we spot a community with lifeblood?

1. God is at the center. One of the hallmarks of a lifeblood community is that everyone has the same goal—to put Christ at the center. Those in a lifeblood community want to advance the cause of Christ, and they allow few distractions to that goal. Conflicts will take place. Yet, like the spokes on a wheel, everyone is connected to the same hub and has the same vision to see Christ glorified.

2. Your abilities have value. I've written leadership articles about this topic many times. Great leaders know how to bring out the best in everyone on a team. In that same sense, a community brings out the best in each person. A community thrives when each person is valued and the goal is to have everyone serve in a role in which they can best use their gifts and abilities.

3. The support is real. The concept of supporting each other in a community (or in a church) must be real. It's not just a mission statement on a plaque somewhere. It's not a quickly forgotten platitude. When one member is hurting, everyone responds, like the EMTs at Camp Shamineau. The members are quick to act but never quick to judge. The community is built on the concept of supporting one another and won't take sides or pick favorites.

4. It's attractive. Like the city on a hill mentioned in Matthew 5:14, a lifeblood community will gleam like the morning sun. Everyone will know about it. People will be drawn to the community and want to become part of it. If the lifeblood is at a Christian college, enrollment will go up. If it's in a city where Christians are known for helping the poor and meeting each other's needs, people will want to move there. If it's on the mission field, people will come to Christ. A lifeblood community has an aroma, a sweet scent that draws in the masses.

STUDY QUESTIONS

1. What are the signs of a lifeblood community?
2. When do you know the lifeblood is not flowing in a community?
3. When have you been part of a community like that?
4. What did you like about it?
5. What's a specific example of you being supported by a lifeblood community?
6. Are you in a lifeblood community right now? Why or why not?

AFTERWORD

While I was writing this book, something strange happened. I went to the doctor for a routine physical, and a blood test revealed a problem. There were some signs I might have cancer, and it freaked me out a little. There wasn't much to go on—I would need to get more blood tests and an MRI, followed by a biopsy—and the doctors weren't too sure about my prognosis. They kept telling me not to worry. (I learned that the more a doctor tells you not to worry, the more you should probably think about worrying.)

The irony is, of all the spiritual tests I've had in life, this one was right up there at the top. I was tested when I was at that Christian camp—when my wife was due with our first child, and then we found out we were terminated from the camp and had to move in with my parents. I was tested when I started a music career and discovered that I was operating under my own power and abilities (such as they were). But this new test—which was all about a blood sample during a routine physical—was different. I'm not exactly squeamish, but I'd never been in the hospital before. I'd certainly never had an MRI or a biopsy, and I'd never had to wonder if I might have cancer.

Over the course of several months, leading up to when this book was due to the publisher, I lived in a state of uncertainty. I didn't know what to expect. After the MRI, a doctor identified a dark area in one of my organs. Then, after the biopsy, the same doctor gave me good news: I didn't have cancer. (I do have to get a new blood test every year.)

I do realize that there is some irony here. I've written a book about blood and during the entire writing and editing process, I've had something *in my blood*. No one knows what it is. It's a sign that something is wrong and I may need medical treatment. The other possibility is that there isn't anything wrong with me at all, even if the doctors keep doing tests.

The exciting part of this is that I've passed this new test—both blood and spiritual. Over these last few months in 2017 and the first part of 2018, I've trusted that, no matter what happens to me, God will get the glory. No matter how each new blood test turns out, I can trust that God has a plan. I haven't worried, and I haven't become angry or uptight. If anything, this test has taught me that life really is found in the blood, as it says in Leviticus 17:11. (Another irony: I didn't know about that verse until a few months ago when I heard a pastor mention it in passing. It was long after I named this book and picked the topic. I'm living in a lot of ironies right now.)

I've also seen how God continues to teach me about lifeblood. When you write a book, you become a learner as well. During the entire writing process, God kept speaking to me about what lifeblood really means. Verses I've known for years or even decades came alive. I kept thinking, *Wow, that verse is about lifeblood. So is that verse and this other verse*! I guess it's the opposite of writer's block. It's a writer's flood. The ideas keep coming, even though the book is done. I plan to keep researching what the lifeblood means; I plan to keep learning. I can't tell you that I have the perfect answers, especially since none of this is meant to be a formula.

Once, when I was working with an agent for this book, I was asked about why the book is not more practical. Why wasn't I writing a how-to book when that's what people really want? I don't believe there is a prescription for being a Christian outside the Bible. We place ourselves in the path of God's grace. That's it. We're conduits and vessels. When we sin, we block the flow of blood and become spiritual cripples. We want things to be more cerebral than that. (Maybe we want them to be more complicated, so we can provide the answers and feel good about ourselves.) But it's not complex. In my experience, it's only when we identify and become propelled by the true source of power that we can grow spiritually.

Do you know the difference between an artery and a vein? An artery carries blood away from the heart to the body. A vein carries blood from the body back to the heart. I can't think of a better example of what it means to live a holy life. Our hearts are changed by the transformation we experience through the blood of Christ, and the blood moves out from us to anyone who will listen. Because of this changed heart, we can be holy. Then we receive spiritual nourishment from others back to our own hearts. That happens in marriage, with our kids, and in a community. It's a continual process. It's a cleansing process. It's awesome. We need each other. We need this transfusion. Without it, our hearts grow sick.

God has a plan for whatever is going on with my blood. Maybe it's not serious at all. I know He has used all the testing, poking, and prodding as an example. Either we carry the lifeblood of Jesus or we don't. If we choose to abide in Him, His blood will abide in us. What is flowing inside us, from a spiritual standpoint, either provides nourishment or spreads like a cancer, inhibiting the outpouring from our changed hearts. True spiritual healing means the blood of Christ will miraculously transform us. There will be no sin in us. We will experience light and momentary affliction in this life, but we have the blood of Jesus to sustain us. After that, we will be absent from the body and present with the Lord. So be it.

What is your spiritual condition? Are you trusting that Christ can transform you? Are you trying to bring about the transformation yourself? Are you trusting in your own abilities? Or do you believe that Jesus can radically revitalize your soul?

As I was finishing this book, a tornado touched down near my house. It made the local news because it was the earliest confirmed tornado ever recorded in Minnesota. In March, we usually have snow, not storms. Driving home after walking our dog, I could see the funnel cloud forming. I turned the car around and headed the other way. I had to think about what that means in spiritual terms. At times, we have to do an about-face, meaning that we stop, turn around, and go in the opposite direction in one swift move. *About face* is a military expression, but it applies to our Christian lives as well. We're not quite on the best path; so we slam on the brakes, put the car in reverse, circle around, and drive the other way.

That day in March, I looked behind me and saw a furious wind. Trees were bending over—one looked as if it had fallen on the very road I was on at the time. We never know what is ahead of us. A tornado is a powerful force, but God is an even more powerful force.

Maybe now is the time for you to turn around. I know it's not easy. Once we've been transformed, we must decide to live in such a way that we keep relying on God's power and keep trusting that the Lord will transform us more each day. Communion is not only on a Sunday at church. It's not just a service administered by a pastor with wafers and juice. It's a daily refreshing, a daily washing, a daily administration. God reaches down and taps our hearts, and out pours new blood in our veins that gives us the power to live for Him. Will you?

NOTES

Chapter 2: The Lifeblood in Our Friendship

1. Ed Phelps, "What About Friendship?" Pocket Awareness, October 31, 2016, http://www.pocketawareness.com/what-about-friendship.

Chapter 5: The Lifeblood in Our Jobs

1. John Brandon, "This 7-Minute Morning Routine Will Change Your (Work) Life," *Inc.*, May 19, 2015, https://www.inc.com/john-brandon/this-7-minute-morning-routine-will-change-your-work-life.html.

Chapter 6: The Lifeblood in Our Parenting

1. "Fishing the Lessons from a Simple Pleasure," *Minnesota Conservation Volunteer*, January/February 2003, 42, https://webapps8.dnr.state.mn.us/volunteer_index/past_issues/issue_pdf?issue_id=55.

Chapter 7: The Lifeblood in Our Communities

1. JJ Heller, "You're Not Going Crazy," *JJ Heller* (blog), January 11, 2017, https://www.jjheller.com/blogmenu/2017/8/18/youre-not-going-crazy.

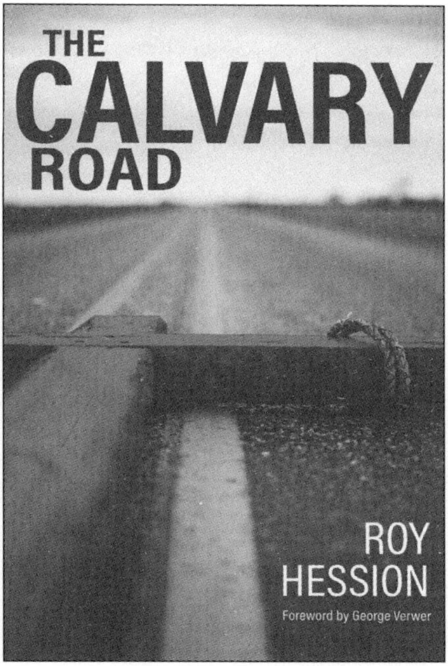

THE CALVARY ROAD

Roy Hession

Do you long for revival and power in your life? Learn how Jesus can fill you with His spirit through brokenness, repentance and confession in this updated version of Hession's classic, *The Calvary Road*. In the course of eleven chapters, Hession emphasizes the need for personal revival in life with Christ.

Paperback
Size $4^{1}/_{4}$ x 7, Pages 162
ISBN: 978-1-61958-226-2
ISBN (*e-book*): 978-1-61958-227-9

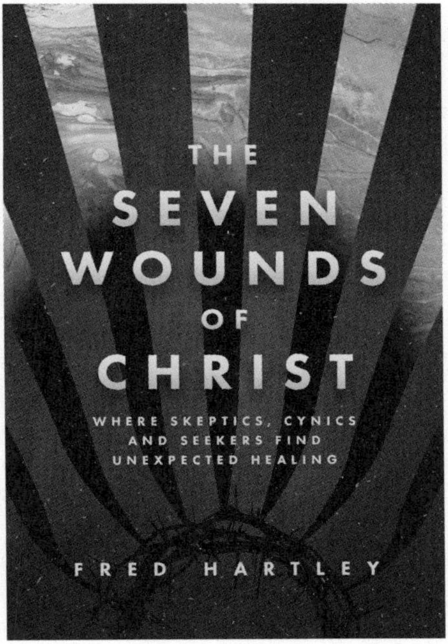

THE SEVEN WOUNDS OF CHRIST

Fred A. Hartley III

Fred Hartley's *The Seven Wounds of Christ* shares how Christ's wounds on the cross represent the fullness of His atonement and how, individually, each wound corresponds to a distinct healing for us. Using straightforward scientific explanations, real-life stories and biblical truths, Hartley teaches that no matter the depth of our wounds, the wounds of Jesus go deeper—and His wounds are for our healing.

Hardback
Size 5 x 7, Pages 151
ISBN: 978-1-61958-258-3
ISBN (*e-book*): 978-1-61958-259-0

SURRENDER

John Stanley

In Surrender, John Stanley encourages readers in the call upon every Christian's life to daily die to self and surrender—in salvation and in every single circumstance. Expertly weaving together Scripture, personal anecdotes, and a white-water rafting story, John explores what a truly surrendered life can look like, and how that provides a new outlook on what it means to live a satisfied, joyful life.

Paperback
Size 5 1/4 x 8, Pages 175
ISBN: 978-1-61958-284-2
ISBN (*e-book*): 978-1-61958-285-9